I have seen Sheila the mom and the incredibly busy superstar executive in action. Sheila says: You can have both. I agree! I observed her perform both roles successfully and am confident you can too. She shares her stories, reflections, and some of her hacks as well. Great lessons in parenthood and business which can co-exist to the benefit of your family and your career. Read the book—your family and your boss will appreciate it.

Randy A. Garfield
Board Member, Sr. Exec Coach, Former President Walt Disney Travel &
EVP Worldwide Sales & Travel Operations, Disney Destinations

What an important read and one made richer by Sheila sharing her personal stories. If you're a woman or mom, read this book now! You will conquer your fear and misperceptions about working and raising a family. Bring your best self to everything you do and take the time to celebrate your success and impact!

Amy Cappellanti-Wolf
SVP, CHRO, Symantec Corporation

This is a must-read for every woman who wants to be their very best. Sheila's message encourages women to enjoy their lives a lot more and give themselves a break. As the owner of my own estate firm, it is hard to build your career and balance time with your family. Work gives a woman so much self-empowerment, and that's step one in empowering those around her.

Kim Bergin
Broker, Clermont Lakes Reality

Each day, we strive to inspire the 1000s of women at GE to take charge and own their careers. Sheila's empowering story shows that you can have a job at any level, raise a family, and succeed as an executive in a large corporation.

Nasrin Rezai
EVP, Chief Information & Product Cyber Security Officer, General Electric

Sheila Jordan inspires with personal stories as she raises a family despite the challenges that come with a global and incredibly successful career. Sheila's beautiful story encourages women to pursue their personal and professional dreams and not be afraid to have it all! As a mother of three young children, hearing from Sheila's grown children reaffirms my shared commitment that wherever I happen to be, I will be all in!

Alvina Antar
Chief Information Officer, Zuora, Inc.

I knew when I met Sheila Jordan at our daughters' basketball practice that I had found my soulmate - balancing roles as wife, mother and hard charging executive at Cisco. Over the years, Sheila and I have shared the joys and tears of parenting. No one is more passionate about her work and committed to her family than Sheila. I'm thrilled she's sharing her lessons learned with the next generation of moms.

Sue Bostrom
Former EVP & CMO, Cisco Systems
Corporate & Private Board Member

In my personal experience as Sheila's niece and goddaughter, I have seen her in many of the real life situations she shares in this book. As a mom, I learned a lot by watching her in action and you're in it for a treat. You'll see Sheila in action like I did and learn her disarmingly insightful approach to raising her kids and pursuing her career.

Jessica Jensen
Product Marketing Specialist, Rollins College

As mothers, we are our toughest critics as we raise our kids, take care of a career. We are shaped up by the choices we make every day. Sheila shares her stories, tips, and invites us to make our own choices and learn by doing.

Ginna Raahauge
Chief Technology Officer, Catholic Health Initiative

YOU ARE NOT RUINING YOUR KIDS!

A Positive Perspective on the Working Mother

Sheila B. Jordan

YOU ARE NOT RUINING YOUR KIDS!
A Positive Perspective on the Working Mother

Copyright © 2018 by Sheila B. Jordan

All rights reserved. No part of this publication may be reproduced, distributed, or transmitted in any form or by any means, including photocopying, recording, or other electronic or mechanical methods, without the prior written permission of the author, except in the case of brief quotations embodied in critical reviews and certain other noncommercial uses permitted by copyright law. For permission requests contact the author.

Limit of Liability/Disclaimer of Warranty: The publisher and the author make no REPRESENTATIONS or warranties with respect to the accuracy or completeness of the contents of this work and specifically disclaim all warranties, including without limitation warranties of fitness for a particular purpose. No warranty may be created or extended by sales or promotional materials. The advice and strategies contained herein may not be suitable for every situation. This work is sold with the understanding that the publisher is not engaged in rendering legal, accounting, or other professional services. If professional assistance is required, the services of a competent professional person should be sought. Neither the publisher nor the author shall be liable for damages arising here from. The fact that an organization or website is referred to in this work as a citation and/or a potential source of further information does not mean that the author or the publisher endorses the information, the organization or website may provide or recommendations it may make. Further, readers should be aware that Internet websites listed in this work might have changed or disappeared between the time this work was written and the time it is read.

To contact Sheila:

Email .... WorkingMomsJordan@gmail.com

LinkedIn .... https://www.linkedin.com/in/jordansheila/

Twitter .... @SheilaJordan90

To contact the publisher, inCredible Messages Press, visit www.inCredibleMessages.com

Printed in the United States of America

ISBN 978-1-7322510-2-1 paperback

ISBN 978-1-7322510-3-8 eBook

Book Coach .... Bonnie Budzowski

Project Management Team .... Leslie A. Rubin and Ash Seddeek

Cover Design .... Bobbie Fox Fratangelo

Illustrations .... Suzanne F. McGinness

DEDICATION

TO MY DAD, MY HERO AND THE PERSON who has helped make me who I am today. My dad showed me the way. He taught me hard work. He taught me to stand up for myself and my beliefs and what's right. He was supportive with unconditional love, and he loved me to the moon and back.

That love catapulted me in ways I would have never dreamed possible. That love and support is part of my DNA. It is what fuels me in being a mother. Sure, there are times when discipline is required and the tough conversations. My dad always taught me that discipline is also a form of love.

I lost my dad here on earth on May 22, 2018 to the horrible disease of Alzheimer's—but he remains in every fiber of my being and in every page of this book. For those of you who still have your parents alive today: Put this book down and call them right now. They live for those calls. If you haven't spoken to your parents in a long time, forgive and call them. Then come back and read the book that will hopefully change your life.

ACKNOWLEDGEMENTS

SO MANY PEOPLE HELPED SHAPE ME into the person I am, which has allowed me to be a professional working mother.

My bosses. I'm grateful for the endless feedback you gave, even when I didn't want it. Your deep desire and commitment to simply make me better has made a huge difference in my life. Your courage in explaining better ways to approach things has made me a better problem solver and a better leader. Your honesty throughout the years is simply a gift.

My friends throughout the years. We laughed until our bellies hurt, we cried, we talked, and talked, and talked. We went to school together. We worked together. We partied together. We raised children together. We drank wine! You allowed me to let me hair down and simply be me. We learned together. We grew together. I so deeply cherish each of you.

My friends who agreed to be interviewed for the book. Kim, Kaki, Joanne, Gwen, and Dierdre, your input made this a better book.

Mom and Dad. Thank you for being positive role models, for creating an amazing family environment, for always believing in me. You brought me up by truly believing I could be anything I wanted to be. Anything.

Phil. My husband. My champion. My life partner and my rock. There is no one else I would choose to spend my life with.

My sisters. We couldn't be more different, and yet I know you are only a phone call away for anything. I cherish our life together, and I am so happy you both are older than me… always!

My children, all of you. This book is about you and for you. While I have been so blessed with so many things and accomplishments in my entire career, single biggest accomplishment and my single biggest source of pride is each of you. My heart sings when I see you. My eyes fill up with both joy and tears when you are happy or sad. I simply could not love anyone, or anything, more than I do you. A gazillion red Swedish fish is how much I love you.

My book project team. Leslie Rubin, Bonnie Budzowski, and Ash Seddeek, without your insight and guidance, this book would never have been completed. Our Friday conversations and back-and-forth drafts were invaluable. Susan Nystrom, you arranged countless phone meetings and juggled my schedule. I appreciate your organizational skills.

My readers. My wish is this book allows you to see that you can have a meaningful career while raising children. My hope is that you will laugh at a few stories and see that humor is a great stress release. I hope you can reduce any guilt that you carry and replace it with conscious intent as well as with the deep knowledge that by choosing to work, you aren't ruining your kids. You are indeed offering an incredible positive experience for your children, even if some days don't feel that way. You are also sharing your giftedness with the world and modeling for your children how to make the world a better place.

CONTENTS

FOREWORD 1

WORKING MOTHER:
REWARDING, CHALLENGING, AND MAGICAL............................ 7

WORK/LIFE BALANCE:
USELESS PURSUIT 21

PERFECT COMBO:
CHORES AND BROADWAY MUSIC 33

KEEP THINGS LIGHT:
THE GREAT SOCK SECRET 49

FLEXIBILITY AND INFLEXIBILITY:
WHEN AND WHERE? 61

KIDS ARE ALWAYS LEARNING:
THE M&M DISASTER.. 71

KEEPING CONNECTED:
CAR TALK AND RESPECTFUL STALKING.............................. 85

ONE JOB COMPLEMENTS ANOTHER:
FOR BETTER AND BETTER... 99

CONVERSATION WITH MY ADULT CHILDREN:
PERSPECTIVES FROM THEN AND NOW 113

LOOKING BACK, LOOKING FORWARD:
THE PRINCIPLES STILL STAND...................................... 131

ABOUT THE AUTHOR... 139

FOREWORD

THERE'S NO SHORTAGE OF PROFESSIONAL WOMEN juggling work with their role as a mom—admirable women who are committed to bringing their best to both jobs. There has been, however, a shortage of books that speak to the realities of this challenge from someone who has lived it—at least until Sheila Jordan put her fingers on the keyboard. *You Aren't Ruining Your Kids* is going to be one in a million in its category.

We know this because we are two professional women who now have grown or nearly grown children. We know what a long, welcome, and wonderful journey raising kids while you work can be. Allow us to introduce ourselves.

Ana Pinczuk is Senior Vice President and General Manager of Hewlett Packard Enterprises Pointnext Services. She worked with Sheila at Cisco, where she was a senior executive in services and engineering roles. Diana McKenzie spent 30 years in the life sciences industry, almost all in IT roles. Currently she is Senior Vice President and CIO at Workday. Diane first met Sheila at a dinner hosted quarterly for women CIOs in the Silicon Valley.

When Sheila, now Chief Information Officer at Symantec, told us she was writing this book, we were both excited and reflective. As a working mom, you go through many emotions: fierce love, nagging guilt, pressure from others' expectations, and the determination to give your children and your job the attention they both deserve. To succeed, you have to decide what's important to you and pursue that with singular purpose. At both work and home, you have to define your mission, your North Star, and then judge and adjust the course of your life in relationship to that North Star. And no one has the right to tell you what True North is for you. It's different for everyone.

Sheila's premise is that kids of working moms thrive. They are likely to be more independent and possess more developed skills of planning, prioritizing, and problem solving. Sheila makes you laugh with stories about how she managed stressful situations and how, in the end, her kids developed a sense of self and responsibility.

Sheila offers all working moms a break when she declares that striving for work/life balance is a useless pursuit. Life is fluid, and on some days, work will take priority; on other days family will. Sheila effectively makes the case for striving to integrate rather than balance work and family.

At the same time, Sheila is abundantly clear about her commitment to holding certain family times, such as celebrations and vacations, as sacred. When her kids were little, Sheila would do whatever was needed to ensure they had her undivided attention in the evenings and at bedtime. You'll enjoy reading about how her team at work misread her working habits as an expectation that they answer calls at 3 a.m.

We stand with Sheila in the view that asking for help is a sign of wisdom and a search for win/win outcomes. Help can come in the form of trading and bartering with other parents—picking up kids from sports, for example. If you can afford help, get it. Get over any guilt and use help to get the more mundane things out of the way, so that you can focus on the more important aspects of parenting. This book contains some interesting suggestions and examples.

Many of Sheila's stories involve intentional rituals that strengthened the bonds of her family. The rituals range from securing colored M&Ms to match party themes, to creating an elaborate New Year's Eve practice of reflecting on the highs and lows of the year. In Sheila's family, lighthearted fun mixes seamlessly with the intent to encourage and hold each other accountable to continually learn and improve.

As working moms, we've recognized the importance of rituals in our families, too. Assuming neither parent was traveling, Diana's family ate dinner together. Sometimes dinner didn't happen until 8 p.m., but it involved a conversation in which each family member shared his or her high and low point of the day in a meaningful way. (Kids weren't allowed to say recess was the day's high point.) Those daily conversations kept the family vulnerable and close. Diana and her husband told the highs and lows from their workdays, which allowed the kids to see that their parents were people with challenges as well as adults who seemed to have all the answers. The family dinner ritual was similar to a game Sheila calls roses and thorns.

Ana is from Argentina originally, and her husband is from Iran. Because she traveled for work, Ana was not always home for dinner. She declared Fridays as her sacred family day. For 20 years, Ana's family has designated Friday as the time to gather with other couples and enjoy Persian food. Their children know that the family will be home on Friday evenings and that various people will drop by. It's a special time, and a tradition everyone can count on.

So much of healthy family life is about connection and staying in conversation when things are going smoothly, and especially when they're not. No matter how busy you are, you need to carve out time to talk. This has never been truer than in today's hyper-connected world.

We wish we had known about the car talk strategy Sheila and her husband Phil used when the kids were growing up. The car was the designated space where anyone could ask questions, share concerns, and give information without repercussion. The physical dynamics that preclude eye-to-eye conversation made it easier to talk about awkward or embarrassing topics. What was said in the car was addressed in the car and stayed in the car.

There's so much in this book that you'll want to start reading right away. From the start, you'll be struck and inspired by Sheila's blend of intention and levity. She's very serious about parenting and about her role as CIO of Symantec, but both are communicated in the context of her commitment to live every day to its fullest. She reminds us, "Wherever you are, be all in."

Working moms are driven and goal oriented, and it's easy to get lost in that. Let Sheila remind you, "If no one is getting hurt, and nothing valuable is getting broken, look for the humor in any situation. When humor is not the right answer in a specific situation, stepping back to view that situation from a big perspective nearly always is."

Ana Pinczuk
Diana McKenzie
June, 2018

CHAPTER 1

WORKING MOTHER:
REWARDING, CHALLENGING, AND MAGICAL

I REMEMBER A DAY when my daughter, Jacqueline, was two years old. Dressed in a business suit, I was walking my daughter to the babysitter while she clung to me sobbing, "Don't go, Mommy. Don't go!" Jacqueline was so upset that I couldn't bring myself to leave, yet I had to go to work. I hung around outside for a bit, crying, mascara streaming down my face. After about 10 minutes, I peeked in the window and saw Jacqueline in the center of a group of kids, laughing and bouncing a ball. She was fine, but I was a mess. As the mom of two young kids and CIO at a demanding job, guilt was my steady companion.

If you are a working mom, you know what it's like. You love your kids more than you thought was humanly possible. Naturally, you want to give them the best in every category. Physically, emotionally, educationally, and financially—you want your kids to have a better start than you had. How that better start should look isn't always clear, but in your family, it involves you going to work. Often, going to work can leave you feeling torn between your love for your kids and your professional responsibilities.

For example, if the baby has a fever, you typically still must go to work or meet that important client. It doesn't matter if your mother, husband, or a perfectly competent caretaker is there to care for your child. You are the mother, and you want to be there. Then there are the looks you get when you bring store-bought cookies to the school bake sale, or you happen to forget the cookies altogether. You feel the eyes of the teachers or stay-at-home moms and hear them silently accusing, "You are ruining your kids!"

If you are a single working mother, the tension and struggle can be worse. I know this because I supported a job change for my husband, Phil, in which he worked in California for a year while I spent a year with the kids in Florida. This seemed the best arrangement while Phil tested out a new job and location before we decided to make the move permanent.

Phil came home every other weekend, but the times in between were some of the longest weeks and months of my life. It's better that most people didn't see how I ran the household in those days. Let's just say I let a few things go. For example, Mondays through Thursdays, the picture-perfect family dinner didn't happen, and it didn't matter. We created unconventional dinner times and experiences, such as picnics in bed. In the end, Phil came back to Florida, and I gained a deep appreciation for how difficult it is to be a single working mother—and I only played the role for a year.

I'm on the other side of parenting now. Spencer, my oldest, and Jacqueline are both in their early 20s. Shannon and James, our children from Phil's previous marriage, are in their 40s. Shannon and James (whom I still call Jimmy) lived with their mother, Patty, in California, while the younger kids were growing up in Florida, but they were always an important part of our lives. We got all the kids together when we could, even if only on vacations and holidays. Currently, we all live in California and do many family activities together. All four kids get along well. Each is a wonderful adult, with character traits and accomplishments that make me tremendously proud.

The premise of this book is that you can succeed at both raising your children and having a career. I'm not saying it will be without its challenges. I am saying that you can successfully navigate your way through your parental and professional roles. I'm also saying that in Spencer and Jacqueline, I see distinct strengths that stem directly from being raised by a working mom. As working moms, it's our right to embrace the positives.

To make the book richer, I interviewed some moms who know me well and whose own parenting skills I respect. You'll find some of their stories and tips throughout the book.

To test my premise that children benefit from growing up with a working mom, I interviewed Spencer and Jacqueline about their perspectives and experience as they look back on their childhoods. After all, the proof is in the pudding. You will find Spencer and Jacqueline's input scattered throughout the book, and you'll see that Chapter 9 is devoted completely to them.

Spencer graduated in 2015 from Chapman University and is now a sales account manager at DELL/EMC. He is a natural extrovert, and I believe the exposure to business ideas, skills, and interactions connected to my jobs throughout his childhood contribute to Spencer's current success.

Jacqueline graduated from the University of Connecticut in 2017, where she received a scholarship for Division 1 Lacrosse. Jacqueline's choice to major in management information systems was sparked by her knowledge of my career. She now works for Deloitte Consulting.

Shannon and James are both married and work in pharmaceutical sales. Shannon and Joe have two children, and

I'm delighted to be called Grandma by Samantha and Nicholas, both in elementary school. Our whole family recently joined James and Kristina in welcoming their first child, Valentino Isabella. We couldn't be more thrilled.

Both Spencer and Jacqueline chose to be active in sports as they were growing up and benefited from the discipline required. They actively used the time between dismissal from school and when Phil and I returned home by participating in a variety of sports and becoming exceptional student athletes.

Spencer chose to play football during his college years, and his Chapman football team won the entire regional championship for the first time in Chapman's history when Spencer was a senior.

Jaqueline chose to play lacrosse in college. She was recognized as one of the few lacrosse team members to play in every single game in her entire four years. Despite injuries, Jaqueline never missed a game. She was selected to play in the IWLCA (Intercollegiate Women's Lacrosse Coaches Association) senior all-star game, which is comprised of the top seniors of all the division 1 women's lacrosse players. Both kids did well academically, too.

Raising my kids as a working mom has had advantages for me as well as for my children. For one thing, the experience has made me more self-aware and empathetic. These are good qualities in any environment. And my positive experiences and outcomes have led me to write this book.

I am eager to dispel some of the myths that plague working moms. I am also eager to share some of the innovative and creative things I did to relieve stress and add some fun to parenting.

By describing the positives that working moms bring to the family, I don't intend to suggest that stay-at-home moms are in any way deficient. As a working mom, I've been a target of the internal guilt and external judgment that comes from our culture, a culture in which stay-at-home moms have been the ideal for decades. Countless moms who are in the work world for a variety of reasons fear that they are ruining their children.

We read about how children need their parents, especially during those early preschool years. Of course, kids need their parents at every age, but life isn't that simple. Many parents need two incomes to pay the bills. Most single moms have no choice but to work. Some moms have invested heavily in developing a career path and/or are uniquely gifted to contribute to an organization that serves others. Some moms simply want to work because working provides a sense of fulfillment and accomplishment for them. All these moms love their children with a fierce and enduring love.

Whatever your reasons for being in the workforce, this book is for you. My goal is to share a fresh perspective as well as practical techniques to help you successfully manage your life as a working mom. I believe it's time for a book to say, "Hey, your role as a working mom has advantages for your kids as well as for you."

Together, let's explore ways you can embrace your reality and perform your best at both jobs—while raising happy and responsible kids whom you can be proud to call your own. Of course, you will make mistakes, but that's because you're human. You'd make mistakes in any parenting choice you made. You don't need to feel bad for being human.

I'm not sure there's anything special that qualifies me to write this book, other than my passion and the fact that I've successfully made it through to the other side. My young adult children are responsible citizens who are successfully navigating their own lives. I want to proclaim, "I had a career and did not ruin my kids in the process! You can too!"

My senior and executive-level jobs have included my current position as Chief Information Officer at Symantec and Senior Vice President positions at Cisco and Walt Disney World. These positions demanded that I become adept at juggling roles and responsibilities. Prioritizing, organizing, and directing are part and parcel of every day—at work and at home.

I want to be clear that I'm not writing with the intention of setting myself up as an "I've done it right and you should pattern your parenting after me" author. I'm well aware that I've made mistakes, and I've had to pick myself up and learn from those mistakes. I'm also aware that every family is different and must find its own path. I simply want to share my story in hopes that it will strengthen your own defenses surrounding guilt and trigger your own resources of creativity and problem solving.

Having had a lifelong commitment to responding to stress with levity and creativity, I have stories to tell. Our household was characterized by a certain amount of silliness blended with hard work. Some of the silliness was a gift from my mom, who taught me that silly is good. During my early years, my mom worked as a server on weekends. I remember her coming home with change in her apron and throwing it up in the air, so we could catch the coins.

In addition to silly, life with Phil and the kids has always been characterized by competition. We are a family that will compete over anything, whether it is a sporting event, who can beat his or her best time at a 5K race, or who has done the best job of meeting his or her New Year's resolutions. Both silliness and friendly, fierce competition are elements in our best bonding memories as a family.

None of this means I haven't been serious and intentional about my job as a parent. Phil and I put our kids first and made sure they always knew we loved them unconditionally. I have thought about the issue of working and parenting for many years, and I have principles as well as practical advice to share. I believe you'll find my story as well as my practical tips helpful as you navigate your own journey as a working parent.

Most of this book is not intended as advice—it's more the story of how I navigated my life as a professional and a mom, with some tips you might find useful. At the outset, however, I want to offer four important pieces of advice:

Wherever You Are, Be All In

Since you don't have unlimited time in any area of life, your path to success is in high-quality time—which is all about being fully present and engaged, especially in those minutes or hours that seem the most mundane.

For example, when driving your kids to school or an activity, it's easy to occupy yourself thinking about a work project. If you do that, your body is with your kids, but you aren't. You are divided, and your attention is diluted. Instead, use that car time to play a game or have a conversation about the things your kids care about. When you get to work, give your full attention to that project.

Make being all in an attitude and commitment for your life; this will increase your productivity, decrease your stress, and improve your relationships. Most important, being all in is fun, and fun times create enduring bonds.

Don't Let Anyone Judge Your Family—and Don't Judge Yourself by Our Cultural Ideal

In American society, we share the unspoken assumption that there is such a thing as the perfect family. In fact, the perfect family is a brand that marketing and media have created. No matter that it doesn't come close to fitting reality, we have a

Leave It to Beaver mental model (from a TV show that aired from 1957–1963) that we try to live up to—either consciously or unconsciously.

June Cleaver, the mother in the show, had a perfectly clean house, impeccable hair, and was always present for her children. She was perpetually calm and unbelievably wise. Her house always smelled of homemade cookies, but she was never overweight. June Cleaver and everyone like her is a fantasy—a marketing creation.

Somehow, no matter how progressive our ideas, some part of us judges ourselves against the cultural standard of the perfect family. And since we judge ourselves, we are vulnerable to the judgment of others. The criticism of others only hurts because we are first criticizing ourselves. We have the power to break that cycle.

GIVE YOURSELF PERMISSION TO LET SOME THINGS GO

The role of a working mom requires constant juggling and prioritizing. In order to give your kids your best, you have to let some other things go. Start by accepting that superwoman is a fictional character—a fantasy. If you try to be superwoman, you won't do your best in any of your roles, and you will be constantly struggling.

I can't tell you what priorities to choose, but I can assure you that letting some things go is essential to your sense of well-being. You might choose to give up the goal of a spotless house, a volunteer activity, or a regular adult-only night out. Once you decide what to let go, return to #1 on this list: don't let anyone judge you. Be especially vigilant against self-judgment, that voice in your head that tells you how things *should* be.

ASK FOR HELP

Another of our unspoken assumptions is that asking for help is a sign of weakness. Generally, men don't ask for directions, and women don't ask for help. Throughout history, women have exhausted themselves in the push to be ideal moms, spouses, friends, and community members. When we added the role of professional to the mix, we didn't remove or lessen any of our other roles. We came to expect the professional woman to be superwoman.

Some women are fortunate to have a great parenting partner and helpful parents, as I did, but they still feel the pressure to do everything themselves. One of the best gifts you can give yourself is permission to embrace your strengths and outsource things that others can do better. Once you accept that it is acceptable, even smart, to ask for help, you can use your creativity to trade, barter, and figure out manageable ways to get necessary tasks accomplished.

Many ways of reaching out for help don't involve money. My friend, Kim Vickery-Bergin's mom, a single mother with the income of a seamstress, is my role model for this. I'll be sharing her story in the coming pages.

These four suggestions, of course, are easier to talk about than to put into practice. My experience tells me making them rules for your life is worth the effort. It's okay to start with small changes—just start today.

WHAT TO EXPECT IN THIS BOOK

This book is divided into chapters that explore various aspects of life—the kind of life that juggles a job and kids—ranging from the misnomer we know as work/life balance to how we teach priorities and independence. In each chapter, I'll share a principle or two that guided my choices and behavior in that particular area. I'll share some of my successes and some of my failures. I also hope to share a smile or two with the stories of how we got things done. Along the way, I hope to provide practical tips to make your load lighter.

My goal in Chapter 2 is to debunk common myths about work/life balance, and the guilt that surrounds that concept. The truth is that work/life balance is a fantasy that doesn't exist and never will. When I think of balance, I picture a scale of balanced weights. The idea of balance assumes you can even out those scales and steadily maintain both sides. That, I'm convinced, will never happen.

A scale is constantly changing, and so is life. While we can't achieve balance, we can achieve integration, in which both our work and home lives get the attention they need. Some hours and days will be all about work. Other hours and days will be all about home. And some days will be completely out of kilter. I've learned that that's okay.

Chapter 3 offers a perspective on time, especially high-quality time, which I've already introduced. While your kids need to understand that they are your priority, they don't need 100% of your time. And here is a critical point: it doesn't matter what you do with the time you spend with your children, as long as you are intentionally doing something together. Work and play can be integrated in ways that help you successfully juggle your responsibilities.

For example, in our house, we mixed fun with Saturday chores by blasting music from Broadway shows while we worked. We still enjoy a good laugh when we remember those Saturdays—and especially when we reflect on how Spencer and Jacqueline both eventually won contests based on their knowledge of Broadway musicals.

Every family has its load of stress, and the dynamic of a working mom just adds to it; your reaction to that stress affects everyone around you. From my point of view, if no one is getting hurt, there's no reason to overreact. This mindset makes every day more bearable, even the day your toddler knocks over a tall display in the grocery store. In Chapter 4, I'll share stories of how I used levity and creativity to defuse stressful situations. When levity isn't the right response to a situation, gaining and communicating a sense of perspective often is. My husband, Phil, is especially good at this.

With Phil and I both working when the kids were young, we were flexible about routines and accepted the fact that sometimes work would spill over into family time. I knew that I'd have to miss some sporting events, or step away to take a call. In this regard, we rolled with the punches. When it comes to vacations and family celebrations, however, we were, and still are, inflexible. In Chapter 5, I'll share my perspective of why these special times must be sacred and are essential to bonding with your family.

It doesn't matter if the events themselves are extravagant or frugal; what matters is that you are fully engaged with the family during this bonding time. You need to be apart from normal distractions, and your devices must be off.

Anyone who spends time around young children knows that kids are sponges. Kids mimic and act out the things they see their parents do, whether that's washing dishes, exercising, or showing affection. This dynamic, which becomes less obvious as kids get older, provides a life advantage for kids of working moms. In Chapter 6, I'll discuss some of these advantages and explore how you can capitalize on them.

Maintaining open lines of communication is an essential parenting responsibility. Creating special "space" for your kids to ask questions and say what's on their minds can help your family achieve open communication. In our family, we used the car as a sanctuary for awkward or difficult conversations.

We found that talking with Phil and/or me facing forward, rather than eyeball-to-eyeball with the kids, reduced awkwardness. In Chapter 7, I'll describe how "car talk" and other strategies helped us get through the teenage years.

Although I didn't always see it when different responsibilities pulled me in different directions, I'm convinced that being a mom made me a better leader, and being a leader made me a better mom. Rather than stealing time and attention from each other, each of my primary jobs made me better at the other—as well as a better person overall.

I bring the skills of task management, problem solving, team building, and conflict resolution home from work. I bring the empathy and compassion I've learned from my kids to work. I'm guessing something similar is true for you. We'll explore and celebrate this reality in Chapter 8.

Chapter 9 is my favorite one in the book. If you are deeply skeptical about children flourishing with a working mom, you might read this chapter first. This is the chapter in which Spencer and Jacqueline tell their side of the story—what it was like for them to have two working parents.

They don't pretend to have always liked my work schedule, but they do appreciate the benefits that came as a result. The benefits began to become especially clear when my kids went to college and noticed how dependent their classmates were on their parents. Spencer and Jacqueline had a sense of independence and confidence, as well as skills that were well beyond those of their peers.

Once you've heard from Spencer and Jaqueline, you'll be near the end of the book. The final chapter will summarize key takeaways and leave you with some questions about how my journey as a working mom might connect with yours.

As I see it, this book is a way to add my voice to the conversation about the challenges, joys, and outcomes that working moms experience. I'm not trying to set myself up as a role model or shining example. I'm simply a working mom with a story to tell. Your story is equally important, and I encourage you to add it to the conversation.

For now, welcome to my story . . .

CHAPTER 2

WORK/LIFE BALANCE:
USELESS PURSUIT

PICTURE A BALANCE SCALE—the kind with weights and measures you might find in an old-fashioned store in the Wild West. Once you have the picture clearly in your mind, imagine yourself drawing a bold red circle around the scale and then marking an emphatic red diagonal slash through the whole thing. Use permanent ink.

This picture symbolizes my perspective on work/life balance. No matter how many seminars or books consultants and coaches put together on the subject, work/life balance is a fantasy. It will never exist in the reality of our lives.

Trying to achieve work/life balance—balance being a sense of equal energy to both sides every moment—is to invite failure and heap guilt upon guilt. Every time I've tried to achieve perfect balance, I've come away feeling that I don't measure up on either side, that I'm not doing anything right. In fact, I think the idea of work/life balance is something that someone made up simply to make us all feel guiltier. There's no such thing as balance.

The metaphorical scale is always changing, often tilting massively like a seesaw. There are days when your family is going to take complete precedence over work, and there are days where work is going to be the priority. Be good with this. It's okay.

Some days will be completely out of kilter, with weights flying every which way. That's okay, too. You can give appropriate energy to both work and home; simply accept that a balanced scale is the wrong metaphor. Spend your energy on work/life integration instead.

A word of caution comes from my friend, Dierdre Spina, mother of two: When integrating work and life, remain on the lookout for *red alerts*, times when it is essential for your job to take a backseat—because your child needs you to stop what you are doing and provide guidance, discipline, or whatever attention is appropriate. A red alert may be the first lie, a first episode of underage drinking, a health problem, or a highly emotional experience. Red alerts are likely to arrive at unexpected times, but they deserve your full attention. Knowing that you are on the lookout for these times can lessen your guilt about events you might need to miss for work reasons.

* * * * *

I remember a time when my approach to integration nearly caused a serious problem with my team members. Spencer and Jacqueline were babies, and I was a senior manager and then a director for Disney.

I believe the hours between 5 p.m. and 8 p.m. really matter to young children. Mornings with kids are chaotic; you have to get everyone dressed and out the door. The hours between 5 p.m. and 8 p.m. constitute the best time you get for dinner, baths, stories, and bonding. It's all you really get on a weeknight.

When Spencer was a baby, I realized that my last meeting at work was typically ending around 6 p.m. I'd walk in the house at 7 p.m. or later and have only limited time with my son. I decided that I needed to draw a line in the sand and say, "I'm going to schedule my day so my last meeting ends at 5 p.m. and I walk out the door immediately after." Obviously, I couldn't manage this every day, but I tried hard to say, "no more" after 5 p.m. That allowed me to focus on Spencer and then both young children during the prime hours of the evening.

I'd leave my briefcase in the car and make that time all about the kids. When I was raising kids, neither parents or children had cell phones to keep them connected to work or school. If the briefcase stayed in the car, interruptions from work did as well. I recognize that it's more complicated for parents today, but I still believe parents need to disconnect and make certain hours all about the kids. Obviously, the kids have to disconnect too.

As the kids' bedtime approached, I would read or tell a story, falling asleep right along with them. I knew I was breaking all the rules about sleeping with my kids, but that's what I did. Instead of musical chairs, we'd have musical beds, rotating beds almost every night.

I'd fall asleep with the kids, and then I'd wake up around 1 a.m. or 2 a.m. and think, "Oh my, it's Sheila time!" The house would be quiet, and I'd feel no guilt about doing whatever I wanted to do. I could clean the pantry or catch up on the work I might have done at my desk if I hadn't left at 5 p.m. the evening before.

At this time, Disney did a lot of communicating by voice mail. During my quiet time in the middle of the night, I'd leave all my voicemails and get ready for the next day. Then I'd go to sleep for a couple of hours and wake up organized and ready to go. This worked reasonably well for me. I failed, however, to anticipate the perception of me this would create for those on the receiving end of the voicemails.

One day at work, a member of my leadership team made a comment to the effect of, "We can't meet your expectations."

I responded, "What do you mean?"

He said, "Well, you're leaving voicemails at 2 a.m. or 3 a.m. What do you do, work around the clock? Our perception is that you expect us to respond promptly at that hour. We don't have the capacity to do that."

I burst out laughing, and said, "Oh my God, I send voicemails in the middle of night because I fall asleep at 8 with my kids every night, reading them a story. I get up later to catch up on work and organize things for the next day."

This event occurred several years ago when people paid attention to time differently. Now work is global, and everyone's online all the time. No one looks at what time anything comes in anymore.

At the time, my team did notice, and they assigned a meaning to my behavior that I didn't intend. This was a big learning point for me: It's fine to draw the line in the sand that works for you, but make sure to communicate what you're doing so people understand your intent and you don't send unintended messages.

On the positive side, this story illustrates the fact that work is a *verb* not a *noun*. Work is something you do. It is not necessarily a place or a building anymore. For most of us, today's technology makes it possible to be out of the office while still completing our work with excellence.

As a Chief Information Officer at Symantec, I need to be available 24/7. The nature of the work demands it. In light of this, I love, love, love, my smartphone. I can stay completely connected to work without being tethered to my desk or office. Because of advances in technology, I can be available and accessible almost anywhere.

When Spencer and Jacqueline got older and played sports, technology was the biggest gift of freedom. I could leave work a bit early and see the kids play.

Did I go to every one of the kids' practices? No. Did I go to every one of their games? No. Did I make as many as I could? Yes. Sometimes I'd have to take a couple of calls or respond to an emergency email on the field. I'd go off and find a quiet place and take a couple of calls, but I didn't miss the whole game. I didn't miss the opportunity to cheer for my kids. To me that is work/life integration.

Of course, not all jobs afford the type of flexibility of place that mine does. If you're in the service business, perhaps as a technician, nurse, or cashier, you are on the clock, and there's not a whole lot you can do to change that. I deeply respect those jobs in which you must remain on location without access to a phone. You have your shift to run and little flexibility around that.

If you hold this type of job, having a strong support system is doubly important. You can't continually call off work when your kids get sick or other things happen. While you must have a strong support system, it doesn't have to cost you a fortune. Seek out friends who can cover for you and do the same for them. Bartering is one solution for rigid, inflexible job hours.

My friend, Dierdre, once again has wise advice. She recommends that all working moms of toddlers join a playgroup, even if it is tough to manage the scheduling. Some of the parents there will become your support group, which Dierdre calls your *squad*. Some of the toddlers will become your child's gold friends, those with whom they will go through childhood. Parents in the group will have similar needs for support for years to come. This is the ideal group with which to create reciprocal relationships.

Another solution is to negotiate. It may not seem so on the surface, but everything in life is negotiable. You can ask your employer for certain exceptions or changes in scheduling. For example, you can ask for adjusted hours if you need to come in at 9 a.m. rather than 8 a.m. because you have to get a kid on the bus. If you need 90 rather than 60 minutes for lunch because you are taking care of elderly parents, you can ask. If you do excellent work, your employer should be willing to accommodate reasonable needs.

By nature, I'm somewhat of a negotiator, in part because I love flea markets and am competitive. Whether I'm at an outdoor market, antique store, or car dealership, I always ask for an additional discount. I think of it as a game.

Even so, I didn't believe that *everything* is negotiable until I heard a lecture a few years ago. I've lost track of the name of the speaker, but I've never forgotten the lecture. The speaker asked, "Do you know that you can actually negotiate the price of shoes at Nordstrom?"

Without hesitation, I raised my hand and responded, "No, you can't."

The lecturer responded, "Oh absolutely, yes you can, and Nordstrom will allow you to."

It turns out that Nordstrom salespeople have the authority to give you some discounts. You can also ask if a specific pair of shoes will be going on sale in the next month. Salespeople are aware of upcoming sales, and they will honor the request for the sale price in advance. You can actually negotiate the price of shoes at Nordstrom. Since I heard the lecture, I've done it. You can do it too.

Everything in life is negotiable. Don't be afraid to ask for reasonable adjustments or flexibility at work.

* * * * *

Work/life integration is more realistic than the idea of balance, and it's also better for your kids. As you know, children are sponges who observe and adopt your behavior and attitudes. You can often see this in their play.

For example, one day when I came home from work, Jacqueline and Spencer, who were 2 and 4 years old at the time, were "playing" at work and emulating my calls and having their teddy bears and dolls have meetings and do certain chores. At the time, I was working in finance, and I heard them say that the spreadsheet was wrong and had to be redone—something I said with some frequency. I'm sure the kids didn't even know what a spreadsheet was, but they were attuned to and absorbing what they were hearing.

Observing their game before the kids realized I was there, I was amazed to discover that Spencer and Jacqueline were playing a game they called "boss." They had named the dolls and bears to match the people I worked with: Linda, my boss, Jim, and Randy. The kids were having the bears and dolls do certain chores.

Without any discussion or lectures, Spencer and Jaqueline had noticed some of the things I did at work, and they acted out their perception of being in a meeting and playing boss. How would they know to do this unless they heard me talk about my job? Unless my job was part of my bigger life? Unless they heard me on calls with my colleagues?

Whatever your job, you give your kids a gift when you bring them into the work aspect of your life, at whatever level they can understand it. The fact that, at ages 2 and 4, Spencer and Jaqueline understood the notion of a boss and what a boss might do is amazing. Over time, Spencer and Jaqueline met the people I worked with. Rather than playing doctor, as many kids do, they played business meeting because that's what they saw me acting out.

As the kids grew, they observed, asked questions, and picked up more and more. They soaked up a positive work ethic, a commitment to excellence, generating in-the-moment solutions, creativity, problem solving, and the skills of planning and prioritizing

We did a lot of entertaining when the kids were young, and they were often around adults. Spencer and Jacqueline also traveled with us as young children. They learned to interact with grown-ups and state their own opinions as well as listen to and respect the opinions of others.

Recently, Spencer, at 23, joined me at a senior executive outing, and he held his own with three senior executives. He was engaging, asked questions about their businesses, talked sports, and simply connected in a natural way. I was proud to watch that exchange.

Both my kids are mature for their age and well equipped for social and business situations. I don't think of my kids as geniuses, but they are seasoned, observant, and able to connect the dots. They are both strategic. I believe that travel and the open conversations and debates we've had throughout their lives were big contributors to these skills.

Of course, you don't have to entertain executives or travel internationally for your kids to benefit from exposure to your work life. Each profession has its own lessons to impart, and every working parent can share a positive work ethic, a glimpse of interaction with colleagues or customers, and the skills of planning and organizing. Sharing your work life (and also your volunteer life) also teaches your kids that the world is bigger than what happens within your own family's four walls.

Give your kids and yourself the gift of integrating your home life and your work life. You'll both be better for it. While you are at it, *reject* the idea of work/life balance.

Okay, so even if you do a great job of integrating your home life and work life, you still have a lot to pack in during limited hours. Is it even possible to give your kids love, security, and a sense of belonging they need from you as mom when so many of your hours are eaten up by work, commuting, business travel, and chores? Is it inevitable that caregivers, teachers, and others who spend so much time with your kids dilute the bond you have with them?

KEY TAKEAWAYS

- **THE CONCEPT OF WORK/LIFE BALANCE IS A FANTASY**
  On some days, your family will rightfully take precedence over your work, and on other days, work will be the priority. When you accept this trade-off, your guilt over being less than perfect in either arena will decrease. Spend your energy on work/life integration and leave the idea of balance behind.

- **THINK ABOUT WORK AS A VERB RATHER THAN A NOUN**
  With today's technology, it's possible to be out of the office sometimes while still completing your work with excellence. If your job requires you to be in a physical space, understand that everything is negotiable. If you need to adjust your hours to get kids on the bus or care for aging parents, ask. People who perform according to high standards deserve flexibility.

- **STRIVE FOR WORK/LIFE INTEGRATION RATHER THAN BALANCE**
  Striving for work/life integration rather than balance is more realistic, and it's better for your kids than striving to keep work and life separate. When you share your work life with your children at whatever level they can understand, they begin to absorb a positive work ethic, a commitment to excellence, and the skills of planning and organizing. Over time, they gain an advantage in these areas.

CHAPTER 3

PERFECT COMBO:
CHORES AND BROADWAY MUSIC

SPENCER STILL GROANS, remembering how he would wake up as a kid on Saturday mornings to the sounds of Andrea Bocelli and Sarah Brightman, knowing the music meant he'd spend the next few hours doing chores. He'd drag himself out of bed as the CD switched to *Cats* and then to *Phantom of the Opera*. Spencer claims he can hear those songs replay in his head to this day. On the other hand, Jacqueline still cleans her space to blasting music. She believes it makes the job easier.

With hectic work lives and the kids' schedules at various ages, Saturday mornings were our only real opportunity to complete household chores. I wasn't going to do the chores by myself, and I wasn't willing for any of us to be grumpy about it either. Whatever we do as a family, work included, can and should be fun.

My idea for fun with chores is to play music, particularly Broadway music—loudly. So, this became our Saturday morning ritual. Once the chores were done, we would typically have half of Saturday and all of Sunday to play together.

Originally, the ritual was designed to manage necessary tasks, but in hindsight, I see that I was also teaching my kids about responsibility. They were learning that we could enjoy working together and then go play together. There are plenty of benefits to doing both together.

When the kids were in high school, many years into the Saturday chore routine, both Spencer and Jacqueline unexpectedly encountered and won trivia contests featuring Broadway musicals. It's funny—and a great illustration of how kids simply *absorb* information and skills as they watch their parents model them. I'm convinced that kids of working moms soak up all kinds of skills, particularly those of planning, prioritizing, and integrating. Mine happened to pick up Broadway trivia, too.

During my own childhood, both my parents modeled a lifestyle that put their kids first. When Phil and I started a family, we made a commitment to do the same. While we both continued to invest in our careers, once we had the kids, we left many of our adult-only activities behind, things like golfing with friends or adult-only dinners. And because our kids were in the care of others during our working hours, Phil and I were more eager to spend time with them than we were for date nights or vacations as a couple.

This doesn't mean we stopped doing enjoyable things; it means we shifted to activities we could share with our kids. For example, when Phil and I went out to dinner, we took the kids. When we entertained for business, we included the kids and asked our business associates to bring their kids. Spencer and Jacqueline learned to converse with adults as well as to enjoy the company of other kids. The exposure to different kinds of people was good for us all. And we made sure it was fun.

When the kids were young, we resided in Florida and were fortunate to live on a lovely lake. We had an old ski boat and used it a lot. We'd take the kids and our friends out on the lake. I can't begin to count the number of kids Phil taught to waterski.

The boat and the lake were great perks, but I don't want the perks to detract from the key message of this chapter: It doesn't matter *what* you do with your kids in the limited time you have with them. The quality of your time and attention is what counts.

Time together, whatever the activity, is about bonding and creating memories. Chore times on Saturdays were as important in bonding with my kids as was ski time on the lake. You don't need unlimited time with your kids (quantity). You need focused time in which you genuinely share activities (quality). In a busy life, this requires creativity more than resources. Every family has chores, and community parks can be as much fun as lakes. Board games offer affordable paths to fun family nights. And, with creativity, you can invent a friendly competition to make any location and situation fun. The icing on the cake, when you do many things together, is that the kids also learn responsibility: chores first and then we all can play.

On workdays, I was sure to focus my full attention on the kids during that precious 5 p.m. to 8 p.m. slot, especially when they were little. A psychologist once told me, "The worst thing you could do is to come home, see the kids, tell them how much you missed them, smother them with hugs and kisses, and then get on a business call or go into your home office and start working. Your kids can actually feel doubly rejected."

Instead, I learned to leave the briefcase in the car and walk (sometimes run) in and loudly proclaim, "Mommy's home. I'm so excited. Everyone's home. We get to be together."

Again, it's an issue of quality versus quantity. I wanted my kids to know they had my undivided attention, that those hours were all about them. We would do homework, play games, or anything else, as long as my attention was on the kids.

Even with quality time, that dinner/bedtime slot is short, and it's natural to be tempted to feel guilty about how little time you have with the kids on workdays. Those of us who were raised by a stay-at-home parent are especially prone to struggle with this kind of guilt.

When Amy Wolf, my friend and colleague at Symantec, shared such feelings with her mother, she got some wise counsel. Amy's mom told her, "Your kids only know what they know. If they know they are going to spend the day with a good caregiver until you get home from work, they don't know any different. Your kids aren't losing something they know about."

She went on to tell Amy, "A lot of the guilt you're feeling isn't about how the kids feel; it's about how you feel—because you feel like you should be there in the way I was for you. You are a different person with different opportunities than I had. So, forgive yourself."

* * * * *

Because of our smartphones, achieving the ideal level of undivided attention is especially hard for parents today, but undivided attention is still essential. I admire one of my friends who has a no-phone policy at dinner. The younger kids, teenagers, and parents all stack their phones in the center of the table because dinnertime is set apart for talk. The family is committed to having a focused conversation over dinner, without phones. This policy is not easy, but it is powerful.

This same family taught us to play a game called roses and thorns, a variation of an ancient spiritual practice. In this activity, each member of the family first talks about the roses (good things that happened) in his or her day. Then each person talks about a thorn or challenge in the day.

This simple game has multiple benefits. It provides an avenue for constant communication in the family, allowing each member to know what is happening in the lives of the others. The kids get to see that even grown-ups have thorns and vulnerabilities.

The game of roses and thorns encourages everyone to appreciate the good things that happen in any given day. And everyone gets to add his or her perspective and advice to the others. Every problem and opinion is valued and respected, no matter how young or old the family member. The dynamic creates a powerful family bond.

Of course, each family is different, and each must create its own rules and patterns that allow for that focused time. In a family in which one parent works shifts, dinner won't be the best point of connection.

Whatever structure or rhythm parents choose for their family, they must have time when their primary message to the kids is, "I'm present for you right now. I'm not distracted. I'm not watching television. I'm not working. Nothing is more important to me than you right now." The structures themselves must be living structures, ones that shift as the kids grow and change.

In the spirit of managing time and doing things together, let me tell you about a stupid decision I made. This was a full-out stupid decision.

During the year that Phil was trying out a new job in California, the kids were still young, and I was in Florida with them. I think I had just gotten promoted to director at Disney, so I had a fairly challenging job.

Clermont, a town 25 miles west of us, featured a chain of lakes, rolling hills (Florida is otherwise flat), and thousands of orange groves. The area was so beautiful that I was aware that the town was going to grow and grow fast.

Phil and I visited Clermont and fell in love. We thought it would be a great place to get in early and raise the family. So, what did I do? I decided that we would build a house.

If you have ever built a house, you are probably rolling your eyes or laughing right now. You could have told me that building a house is a full-time job in itself, and I already had two of those, especially with Phil living across the country.

I am not exactly sure what made me think I could handle building a new home during that time, but I did. Once I was in neck deep, I knew there was no way out except to go forward and get to the other side. I simply went on autopilot and tried to get as much done as humanly possible during the time available.

As the house progressed, I needed to make decisions about materials, lighting, furniture, and more—all on Saturdays. The convenience of the Internet wasn't yet available, and I wasn't willing to leave my kids with a babysitter. Instead, I took Spencer and Jacqueline with me and made shopping an adventure.

Luckily, a local furniture store called Robb & Stuckey served lemonade and homemade snickerdoodle cookies to customers. What a recipe for success! I'd have the kids pick out a board game or grab some action figures from home, and off we would go to Robb & Stuckey's for lemonade and cookies.

The employees loved the kids, the kids loved the whole picnic-like experience, and I'd make a few more of my decisions on each visit. Spencer and Jacqueline laugh at the memory because, at the time, they had no idea we were doing a chore. We were working and playing at the same time— once again integrating, rather than segregating, our lives. Today, when we need to go to the store, sometimes my kids tease me, saying, "Let's go play Robb & Stuckey."

Since playing Robb & Stuckey was my choice every Saturday, I would make a deal with the kids for Sunday. I was fortunate to be working for Disney that year, and if we "shopped" on Saturday, we would spend Sunday morning at the water park, Typhoon Lagoon. Spencer and Jacqueline loved Sunday mornings at Typhoon Lagoon. Since the kids got up early, we'd arrive at the park by 7:00 a.m. and play in the kid pool for hours. We would buy a picnic lunch of peanut butter and jelly sandwiches, which was served, with a Disney kid-friendly flair, in a pail with a spoon. Typically, we'd be home by noon.

Of course, we could have played at home, but I was likely to get distracted by dishes, laundry, or something else. It's hard to have full-out playtime at home. Going out to Typhoon Lagoon was a special event and dedicated time for all of us. As a bonus for me, the kids were exhausted by the time we got home. They would nap for a couple of hours, and I could get things done. I stuffed everything I could into those couple of hours.

$$\star \ \star \ \star \ \star \ \star$$

Each of us is perpetually juggling time. As a mom with a professional career, I felt the pressure acutely every day. Phil and I tried to split our tasks, but even that wasn't enough. In today's ever-changing world, the only constant is a 24-hour day. You get no more, no less. My goal was and is to optimize that time. I always think about how to use the time available in the best possible way, knowing it's impossible to complete everything on my to-do list. We all live with this same impossibility.

The only hope for me—and for you—is to give ourselves permission to let some things go. Before I had Spencer and Jaqueline, my house was immaculate. I was a paragon of organization, to the point that Phil's shirts were organized by color, in the spectrum of the rainbow. Even our garage was clean. You could literally eat off the floor. And then the kids came.

Like all moms, I struggled with the marketing ideal of the perfect family and the superwoman myth. I'm not sure how long I wrestled with these unspoken ideals and the accompanying guilt before I concluded: Making the kids a priority meant I had to let other things go—or live with unhealthy stress and exhaustion. I had the freedom to decide to live with dusty baseboards, unmade beds, and messy closets. No one, in fact, would die from such conditions, at least not if I tidied them up occasionally.

I developed an entirely new list of things that were so much more important than my closet being organized and my baseboards being clean. Standards for the house changed, and the garage temporarily became a storage space. I learned that a shift in standards was okay, and I could give myself permission to let some things go.

I not only learned to let some things go, I learned to ask for help. I can't describe the huge relief that came when I finally embraced the idea that needing and asking for help is not a weakness.

When you think about it logically, outsourcing tasks is the opposite of weakness; it's good sense. It's foolish to expect yourself to be good at everything. And the effort to be good at everything steals precious time from your kids while interfering with your own peace of mind and physical well-being.

You can outsource by paying, or even better, by trading or bartering. For example, if you have a friend who is better at crafts than you are, you might trade help with a crafty school project for dinner or a ride to soccer practice. The opportunities are endless once you are willing to accept that you don't have to be superwoman—and ask for help.

My friend, Kim Vickery Bergin, mother of a blended family of two biological and five adopted kids, has extensive experience in banking. She uses a deposit and withdrawal metaphor to talk about the dynamic involved in getting the help you need to complete all your tasks.

Kim was raised by a single mother, a seamstress with few assets beyond her talent. One day, Kim arrived home from second grade and announced, "Mom, I need an angel costume by tomorrow."

"What!" her mom responded. "Why didn't I know about this before?"

Kim remembers snapping back to her mom, "Well, you should feel good about this. Sally's mom has it worse than you because she and her sister are both angels and her mother doesn't sew like you do."

Here is the amazing thing about Kim's mother: She answered the smart remark by saying, "Do you know Sally's phone number?"

Then Kim's mother called Sally's mother, Maxine, introduced herself, and offered to help make the angel costumes. Maxine volunteered to purchase the materials, and

Kim's mother made three angel costumes in the next four hours.

Although Kim's mother was poor and of a much lower economic and social status than Maxine's family, she didn't let that intimidate her from reaching out and offering to help.

As a result, Kim's mom and Sally's mom became friends and engaged in a long-term reciprocal friendship. Sally's family, having many more resources than Kim's, were generous. In fact, Sally's dad bought Kim her first car and gave her away at her wedding. Kim's mom made Sally's wedding dress and the bridesmaid dresses for her sister's wedding. Kim still refers to Sally's mom as Aunt Maxine.

Kim is quick to point out that her mom made the first deposit into the relational bank account with Maxine. She couldn't know in advance how Maxine would react.

* * * * *

Phil and I found a creative way to get help when the kids reached middle school and began playing sports. We hired a college student for the hours between 3 p.m. and 5 p.m. on weekdays. The student, who didn't have classes during that time slot, drove our kids to and from practices. This was an affordable and wonderful arrangement.

When Phil was living and working in California, the kids hadn't yet reached that point—they were still in daycare and needed a lot more attention and care. When Phil took that job, I knew I would need the help of a nanny to manage my multiple responsibilities. Phil and I cut costs everywhere to be able to afford the expense.

I didn't hire the nanny to do grocery shopping, laundry, or even cooking. Her only responsibility was to take care of the children. This arrangement made it easier for me to have outside help in our home. Others might prefer to have help with household chores as well the kids.

Hiring the nanny allowed the kids to be home with their own toys, where they were most comfortable, and my mornings were less chaotic when I didn't need to drive them to daycare. But it wasn't always like that.

Before I could afford to hire a nanny, I would drop the kids off before I went to work. And nearly every day, I would race to pick up the kids on time.

One part of the back route to the daycare was a 25-mph speed limit. I got five speeding tickets on that stretch of road in six months because I had to be at the daycare by 6 p.m. for pickup. This led to mandatory participation in traffic school for a full week from 6p.m. to 10 p.m., which only added to the stress. Somehow, we got through it.

Needless to say, I know the stress of having to walk out of an intense business meeting or needing to leave the office when someone on your staff needs you or your boss is looking for you, because you *must* pick up your children.

As much help as a nanny or any caregiver can be, I'm guessing that nearly all moms struggle with entrusting their children's care to another, whether it be part time or full time. I worried we wouldn't find the right nanny; I worried that she would be lazy and not really play with the kids. I even worried that the kids would attach to the nanny in a way that displaced me. After all, she had so much *time* with them. The angst was awful.

Today there are many ways to do background checks, referrals, and even video to ensure you get the very best help, but it's still not easy to trust the care of your kids to a stranger for long hours.

I had to accept that quality of time is more important than quantity. I had to let go and trust that I was the mother of my own kids and would always hold that role. I had to acknowledge that it was a healthy thing for the kids to have a bond with their caregiver.

The right arrangement with a caregiver, of course, is unique to each family. Personally, I drew the line at having a live-in nanny. While I wanted and needed help during the day, I didn't want a nanny around when Phil and I were home. I wanted us to be the only parental figures. I simply wanted my kids to myself.

* * * * *

In terms of quality, I came to believe that my kids needed two realities to become firmly rooted in their hearts and minds. First, they needed to know that Phil and I loved them unconditionally, no matter what. Second, they needed to know they had access to us, even when we weren't home.

I needed the nanny's help with this second "root," and I had to course-correct a few times before getting the right fit. This included the understanding that the kids were allowed to call me when they genuinely felt they needed me, when the kids had what *they* perceived to be a crisis. It was the nanny's job to care for the kids, not to put up barriers between the kids and me because I was working.

One afternoon, I was pulled out of a meeting because the kids felt they had an urgent crisis. They were beside themselves, and I received an emergency call. Once I got Spencer and Jacqueline to calm down on the phone, I realized that the problem centered on a massive fight about who got to be the dog in Monopoly.

I'll never forget how badly I wanted to laugh, but the kids were adamant; this was a crisis. Always an on-the-spot problem solver, potential responses raced through my mind. I had no intention of choosing one side or the other, so I said, "I know how badly you both want to play, so why don't we do this: You guys each pick something different, and I'll be the dog when I come home, and I'll play with you."

It worked. They were able to move forward and enjoy their game. More important, they were assured they could reach me when they felt desperate to talk to me about their crisis.

As the kids got older, their definition of a crisis changed, but the need to know their parents were there for the important moments in their lives did not. Phil, whose schedule was much more flexible than mine, made it to most of their sports practices and virtually all their games. In fact, Phil traveled to college games to see the kids play, not only because of the loving message his efforts conveyed, but because Phil enjoyed seeing Spencer and Jacqueline play. It was a sort of hobby for him.

For my part, I was grateful for the technology that allowed me to be at many games and still responsibly perform my job. As I said earlier, I believe that work is a verb, not a place, and today you can work from nearly anywhere. In fact, I am editing this book in real time from seat 15D on a United Airlines flight.

The bottom line is that you can be a mom with a career and create a healthy, unshakeable bond with your kids at the same time. It's about quality of time rather than quantity. Don't let anyone tell you otherwise. And don't let others judge you according to that ideal family our media and marketing moguls have created. At the end of the day, only you know what is right for your family.

Of course, you can make great decisions about time and build reciprocal relationships to help and still experience stress. Life is simply full of pressure. I'm committed to responding to life's inevitable stress with innovation and levity rather than yelling, shaming, or blaming.

KEY TAKEAWAYS

- **UNLIMITED TIME IS NOT THE GOAL**
  You don't need unlimited time with your kids (quantity). You need focused time in which you genuinely share activities (quality). It doesn't matter if those activities are work or play, only that you do them together.

- **FOCUSED TIME SENDS A MESSAGE OF LOVE**
  Of course, each family and each stage of life is different, and each family must create its own rhythms and routines that allow for focused time. If you are the parent of young children, the time between 5 p.m. and the kids' bedtime needs to be sacred. If your kids are older, you have more options. The important thing is to send the message, "I'm present for you right now. I'm not distracted. Nothing is more important to me than you right now."

- **WORKING MOMS HAVE TO CHOOSE THEIR PRIORITIES**
  Making your kids a priority means you must let other things go—or live with unhealthy stress and exhaustion. It's okay to let perfectionist standards for your house and other areas of life go by the wayside for a season. Above all, let go of the notion that the media and marketing image of an ideal family has any roots in reality at all. Judge your family by your family, not by any outside standards.

- **ASKING FOR HELP IS NOT A WEAKNESS**
  You will reduce your guilt feelings significantly when you embrace the idea that needing and asking for help is not a weakness. It's foolish to expect yourself to be good at everything, and the effort to be good at everything steals precious time from your kids. Using your creativity to trade and barter services will make this possible, even if you have a tight budget.

CHAPTER 4

KEEP THINGS LIGHT: THE GREAT SOCK SECRET

IF YOUR FAMILY NEEDS to get two parents and young kids out the door, you know how hectic weekday mornings can be. Getting everybody fed, dressed, and prepared for the day can be stressful. Okay, that's an understatement. Getting everybody fed, dressed, and out the door can be crazy and chaotic. No matter how organized I tried to be, nearly every morning had its share of surprises and struggles.

One struggle involved weeks' worth of trying to negotiate with a three-year-old over—imagine this—her socks. Have you ever found yourself negotiating with a three-year-old just to get out the door? It's pretty hard to win.

Jaqueline had decided she didn't like the seams on her socks, and she refused to put the socks on. She became adept at curling her toes so tightly and determinedly that I couldn't get those toes to uncurl. On some mornings, Jaqueline would hide in her closet so I couldn't find her. We battled every morning, and I was exhausted and drained before I even got to work. I would think, "I can negotiate a $10 million deal, but I can't negotiate with a three-year-old child."

One day, out of sheer exasperation and frustration, I grabbed a pair of scissors, and a strategy formed of its own accord. I said, "Jacqueline, let's have a secret. Do you want your toes to dance all day?"

She nodded yes, a bit apprehensively.

With a flourish, I cut the toes off the socks. Then I opened the sock drawer and cut the toes off every pair. I said, "Now you can wiggle your toes all day long. And it's our *secret.*" Problem solved. The family got out the door, and everyone made it to his or her respective spot on time. From then on, Jacqueline's toes were always free to dance.

You may think it was outrageous of me to ruin perfectly good socks to appease a toddler. In my view, I was choosing innovation over stress. Looking back, I'm pleased with my improvised solution in the midst of a morning rush—but I'm truly proud I thought to make the solution a secret. That's what made a new bond between my daughter and me. For years, Jaqueline delighted in that special secret between us.

When I'm clearheaded and not engaged in a battle of the wills, my first step in assessing any stressful situation includes the questions: Is anyone getting hurt? Is anything irreplaceable being destroyed?

If the answer to both is no, I try my best to choose innovation or levity over panic and drama. I don't always succeed at this, but I know that when something goes wrong and I react, I add an additional level of stress to everyone around me. My children don't need that. My colleagues at work don't additional stress 8either.

I remember another potentially stressful situation in which Jacqueline and I were in a grocery store. She was about three years old in this incident as well. It was a challenging age!

The two of us were at the store around 6 p.m., and I was in a hurry, trying to get ingredients for dinner. I was focused, maybe even frantic, so I didn't notice that a huge display of toilet paper had attracted Jacqueline's attention. In my memory, the pile was 10 or 15 feet high.

Seeing movement in my peripheral vision, I turned quickly and saw the whole pile come tumbling down. I looked at Jacqueline; she looked at me and began crying. Her sweet little eyes were filled with terror, utter panic that she was in terrible trouble. I had a mere second to decide how to react.

I went over and said, "Jacqueline, how fun! Did you decide you wanted to go play and see this thing all topple? Here, let's pick it up together."

Everyone around us laughed and helped pick up the mess. One mother approached me and said, "I have to tell you that the way you handled that situation was the best I've ever seen. This could have been a disaster."

From my perspective, I was lucky that in the mere second, I had to react, my best instinct won. After all, no one got hurt, nothing got ruined, and nobody broke a lot of glass. I was distracted, and my preschooler knocked something down. Neither Jaqueline nor I needed to be ashamed or embarrassed. In the moment, I had the opportunity of making this either a traumatic experience for Jacqueline or a simple lesson of watching what we touch and cleaning up our messes. As parents, we forget how much power we have over how our young children interpret events that happen in life.

I've long been convinced that laughter and lightheartedness make every day easier. Only recently did I realize how much my mother contributed to this perspective. Both of my parents were wonderful role models who taught me loyalty to family, a strong work ethic, and an I-can-do-anything attitude.

My dad was intense and inclined toward perfectionism, and my mom was warm and downright silly—sometimes stupid silly. For example, one-time Mom decided to be Santa Claus and come down the chimney. She got stuck, and we had to call the fire department.

Mom also had a Thanksgiving tradition in which she tried to shine a light on my father as a hero. We lived on a large parcel of land, so we had the room for my mother to send my father out with a hunting gun to shoot our Thanksgiving turkey. To ensure he had success, she would throw out a frozen turkey from the second-floor window. Dad would retrieve the turkey and bring it inside as if he had shot it.

Eventually, Mom decided that the ritual was bruising the frozen turkey. She began to throw a rock wrapped in a grocery bag instead, leaving the frozen turkey outside for Dad to retrieve. Okay, Mom was a bit off the far end of the silly scale, but she taught me to be present in every moment and to find levity in all kinds of situations. I'm grateful for the lesson.

I'm not suggesting that silly is the answer to every stressful situation, but a sense of perspective often is. The year we moved to California, when the kids were in fourth and sixth grade, serves as an example.

I had a challenging new job at Cisco, creating an internal IT department under a tight deadline, and the kids went to a highly academic school. Education was important in our house, and my kids thought of themselves as successful students—until they hit Harker Academy.

We quickly came to understand that Harker Academy wasn't a good fit for our kids. The student body was comprised of super academic achievers, and the pressure was intense. My kids were good students, but they weren't geniuses, and they were interested in sports as well as academics.

Good fit or not, we had enrolled the kids in Harker Academy, and we knew we had to make the best of it, at least for a while. One of my early mistakes didn't make things go any easier for Spencer.

Like any good mom, during the first summer we were in California, I made sure we had the summer reading list in time to get the work done. Spencer was required to read *Beowulf*, so I went to Barnes & Noble and bought a copy. Spencer began to read, and before long, he said, "Mom, I don't know what this means; I have no idea what's going on."

We began to read *Beowulf* together. For three or four weeks, Spencer and I read *Beowulf* together every night, discussing and dissecting each chapter as we completed it. Silently, I was wondering why this had to be so difficult.

During the first week of class, Spencer discovered that I had purchased the wrong version of the book. I had bought the collegiate version of *Beowulf*—the version five years beyond his grade level. The poor kid—having no idea there were multiple versions, I had unwittingly made his first week at school extremely hard for him. At least, Spencer and I now understood why he was having trouble understanding and why he was feeling stupid.

Spencer got through the *Beowulf* debacle and was beginning to get his bearings when a math class got the better of him. The class might have been pre-calculus; neither of us remembers that part. On his first test, Spencer barely passed.

As a result, he became frustrated and stressed. He had always been an A or B student. One evening, feeling like a failure and not knowing what to do, Spencer stormed into the bathroom and began to cry.

Spencer wasn't the only one who had had a bad day. I followed him into the bathroom, and before long, we were both crying. Faced with his frustration over his difficult transition, my own frustration spilled out as well. Jacqueline heard the fuss and joined us in the bathroom. I'm not sure why we all landed in the bathroom, but that's where we were.

Earlier that day, I had sat in a meeting at my new job, feeling very much like a non-contributor. As the conversation swirled around me, I realized I didn't know the meaning of the acronyms flying by. In that moment, I felt anything but smart.

I had spent 15 years at Disney before I took the job at Cisco and we moved the whole family across the country. Because of my long tenure at Disney, I knew the company, the team, and the business models quite well.

The shift from Disney to Cisco was by far one of the hardest changes in my professional career. It involved changing industries from Disney/entertainment/consumer to high tech at the deepest level, as Cisco focuses on the network and infrastructure. Now, nine months into my new job, I was deep into this world and still uncertain of many things. It had struck me that day, as the acronyms went by, exactly how steep my learning curve was going to be.

With all of us weeping in the bathroom, knowing that my decision to change jobs was hurting my kids as well as me, my brain ran quickly through our options. I considered and discarded a series of options. For example, I wondered, "What if I quit this job and we all go back to Florida? What if we pull the kids out of Harker Academy and register them in a different school? What if . . ."

I quickly decided that it was too soon to make any radical decisions. Difficult as this transition was, we simply had to push through it, at least for the time being. But how?

I decided that the best thing to do was reduce the pressure on all of us while we adjusted. We needed to reframe the situation and redefine success. In other words, we had to allow ourselves to be less than perfect, less than A+ students and employees. I declared, then and there, that this would be the year we would celebrate the C grade. There would be no pressure for the kids to strive for As and Bs. We all simply needed a year of transition.

I recognized and accepted the fact that Phil and I wouldn't be getting an invitation to the school honors dinners while our kids were at Harker Academy. In the big scope of life, I knew that building resilience in the face of the challenges of Harker Academy was far more important than seats at that dinner.

Imagine how I laughed when Phil and I did get invitations to those dinners—because our kids had attained top honors in sports! Trust me, we celebrated those honors as if they were the most important ones in the world. We celebrated our strengths and worked on our weaknesses.

* * * * *

Spencer has a vivid memory of our bathroom cry. He maintains that I destressed the situation with vulnerability. I think of it as perspective, empathy, honesty, and getting through a rough year.

The struggle and even the failures we were each experiencing didn't need to be equated with shame, and I'm glad I realized that during my quick analysis in the bathroom. Ultimately, that year was a learning experience that helped us get stronger and develop a fresh sense of determination.

Our family is highly competitive, and failure can be especially stressful for us. No matter what we do, we make it into a competition—and we want to win. It just seems to be the way we are built. A dose of realism and humility every now and then can be a good thing. That year of transition constituted a big dose of realism for all of us. Another came from the sports arena.

During his first year in high school, Spencer made the freshman basketball team. Because Jacqueline had to do everything Spencer did, she played basketball at her school as well. Unfortunately, our children are neither tall nor particularly gifted at shooting basketballs.

Spencer tried out for the team again as a sophomore and was cut. He came home devastated, believing he was facing the end of the world. He had participated in a competition and failed.

Phil managed to put the event into perspective in a way that changed the sports dynamic of our family forever. Phil said to Spencer, "If basketball isn't the right fit for you, let's try something else."

Phil had noticed that the school had a lacrosse team, but none of us knew anything about the sport. Together, Phil and Spencer learned about the sport online, and Spencer decided to sign up. Once again, because Jacqueline was the kind of sister who had to do everything her brother did, she began to play lacrosse as well. At the time, Spencer was a sophomore and Jacqueline was in eighth grade. This sport happened to be a more natural fit for their bodies and abilities, and they both excelled right from the start.

Spencer played varsity lacrosse beginning his junior year, and Jacqueline played varsity as a freshman. Both kids were voted MVPs, and both were recruited to play lacrosse in college. Spencer decided to attend Chapman University in Southern California and focus his athletic prowess on four years of football.

Jacqueline went to college on a scholarship for lacrosse, graduating from the University of Connecticut. At graduation, she was recognized for playing in every single game during her four years at college. She was also selected to the Big East Conference and 2nd team All-Conference, chosen from the top seniors across the Big East. Failure at basketball turned out to be a blessing, once Phil put it into perspective and we were lucky enough to find a better fit.

Levity, innovation, and perspective all have power to destress a situation and allow for problem solving and growth. I also believe in the power of calm and kindness.

Early in my career, I wasn't good at this, and I'm not proud of how I've handled every situation. I've needed patient mentors to help me grow in this area.

Now, whether I'm in a leadership position at work or with my family, I try to remember the famous words of Maya Angelo, "At the end of the day people won't remember what you said or did, they will remember how you made them feel."

When we are upset or stressed, it's easy to say something harsh or hurtful. A mentor used the image of a fence to help me see how damaging such words can be.

Hurtful words are like pounding nails into a fence. Even if you eventually apologize and remove the nails, the damage is lasting. Events that upset us will pass, but the relationships are permanent. We need the relationships get us through. I now try to protect my fences by guarding my words.

Whatever happens on any given day, I hope we both step back and look at the day from a big-picture perspective. I hope we destress with creativity and good humor. Above all, let's be kind to one another.

Of course, it's easier to talk about the importance of perspective, creativity, and good humor than it is to maintain these things in the midst of daily chores and challenges. Celebrations and vacations are opportunities to step away from the daily routine and distractions. Carefully holding such times as sacred allows for renewal, reconnecting, and creating memories that bind a family together and build its resilience.

KEY TAKEAWAYS

- **LEVITY AND INNOVATION BEAT STRESS—IT'S A CHOICE**
  When something goes wrong and we react, we add an additional level of stress to everyone around us. If no one is getting hurt and nothing irreplaceable is getting destroyed, try to choose levity and innovation over stress. You might get an unexpected solution—like taking scissors to a preschooler's socks!

- **MAINTAINING A SENSE OF PERSPECTIVE KEEPS YOU IN BALANCE**
  When humor isn't the right response to a situation, gaining and communicating a sense of perspective often is. Sometimes, when life is full of commitments at work, home, school, and at various sports or activities, normal standards simply can't be met. Try stepping back, looking at the big picture and using your sense of perspective to reframe the situation and bring relief. None of us can achieve the highest standards in every situation on every day. Those standards are for super humans, not real people.

- **FOR BEST RESULTS, GUARD YOUR WORDS AND PICK YOUR BATTLES**
  When stressed, it's easy to resort to harsh words that can damage a relationship. Events that upset us will pass, but the relationships are permanent. Protect your relationships by guarding your words and picking your battles.

CHAPTER 5

FLEXIBILITY AND INFLEXIBILITY: WHEN AND WHERE?

I'VE ALREADY TALKED about the daily juggling of integration between work and home, the daily decisions, and the frequent guilt I had, especially when the children were little: I felt guilty at work, thinking I should be at home, and when I was home, thinking I should be at work. It was constant. Some days worked better than others. Some days were a nightmare.

In light of this, I decided early on in my career that vacations and downtime *really matter*. I mean, they are critical! Vacations allow me some personal unconnected downtime to think and reflect, and more important, they create the opportunity for the entire family to get to know each other again and make memories together.

Fortunately, I absolutely *love* to plan. Organizing a party or vacation is relaxing for me, a de-stressor. So, I've enjoyed spending a great deal of energy planning vacations, so the entire family could enjoy each other's company and bond. I know this is cliché, but I genuinely mean it: For a healthy family and successful career, you must work hard, play hard, and hold vacations and special occasions sacred.

Phil and I both grew up in families with strong work ethics, and we both worked throughout our college years.

We've taught our kids to be all in when it comes to schoolwork as well as the discipline involved in sports.

In our house, if I had to miss dinner or be late because of a work-related event, it was a non-issue. There was no drama around this. Phil and I simply reconfigured things to take care of our multiple responsibilities. That's how day-to-day life with jobs and kids always was for us. I'm sure you also juggle schedules and elicit support to meet the needs of your family while you work. One requirement of the working mom is flexibility about daily routines.

But vacation and celebration times are another story altogether. It doesn't matter if the events themselves are extravagant or frugal; what matters is that you are fully engaged—fully present with the family during this bonding time. You need to be apart from normal distractions, and your devices must be off. I've purposefully taken the family to places lacking connectivity so that we could have conversations and look at each other eyeball-to-eyeball.

If, out of 52 weeks of the year, I have a week or two weeks away with my family, I want every minute to be a quality minute. Likewise, I want every birthday to be special and memorable. I love to surprise people with the perfect present or experience.

Because of my 15 years at Disney, I'm enthusiastic about themes. Who better to teach the art of following a theme down to the tiniest detail but Disney? Typically, I carry the party theme all the way through to the color of the M&Ms! Obviously, a perfectly themed event isn't the point, but the themes are fun.

When the kids' birthdays rolled around on July 10th and August 9th each year, we were going to have a party and do something as special as I could make it. This was my commitment throughout their childhoods, whether I had a tight budget at the time or not. Spencer remembers a year in which he had 15 friends playing flag football in the park as happily as he remembers the time we combined both kids' parties and rented inflatable waterslides for our backyard.

The power of celebrations is all about the intention and attention you put into them. The guest of honor must feel loved, appreciated, and celebrated—not as if no expense has been spared—but that so much thoughtfulness has been behind the celebration. I even have a special hat that the birthday person has to wear—and Phil does the birthday dance, which is something akin to the Pillsbury Doughboy meets Michael Jackson.

I remember one of Jacqueline's birthdays being all about dogs and cats. She had decided that in lieu of presents, she wanted everyone to bring food and other items she could donate to the Humane Society. Jacqueline was featured in the newspaper for that birthday. I was so proud of her giving spirit.

Spencer was in high school when we had a casino-themed party for his birthday. Guests played blackjack and gambled with fake money.

But let's talk about vacations. I use the time away not only to bond as an immediate family, but also to include extended family and friends to create lasting memories. Because we have lived in multiple locations, we have people who are important to us spread all over the country.

When it's possible, I invite "extra" people on vacation. I still remember Jacqueline's reaction when I arranged for a special cousin, Jessica, to surprise her on a trip. Jessica was the older cousin whom Jacqueline idolized at the time, and my daughter cried for joy.

As the kids were growing up, the physical distance between Florida, where we lived, and California, where

Shannon and James lived, created barriers. Even so, I worked hard to get us together for holidays and vacations, and I've impressed on all my children the importance of making it a priority to get together as often as possible.

When Spencer and Jacqueline were in high school, everyone lived in California for the first time. James and Shannon were in southern California and we were in northern California, but we still found ways to get together regularly. As the kids have grown into adults, they have become closer and closer. We are a blended family where no one makes the distinction of stepsibling or stepparent. We are just family, and we all consider our times together a priority. Our four adult children, their two spouses, and our wonderful grandkids all vacation together. I love to be called Grandma!

I know that some people simply arrive on a vacation and let it unfold, but I'm not built that way. When you have a group of people traveling, you need a plan and a way to communicate. I create a clearly organized itinerary, and the kids laugh and roll their eyes. They don't understand that the itinerary is as much for me as it is for the rest of the group.

It's natural for a mom to spend her energy while on vacation making sure everyone else is having a good time, but I take my vacations seriously. I want to relax and enjoy the family, the location, the venue, and simply have fun, too. Carefully planning the itinerary before the trip allows me, the working mom, to vacation too. The magic of bonding happens only when everyone, including the mom, is fully present. And, of course, planning and watching the plan unfold happens to be a big part of the fun for me. If that's not true for you, make the planning itself a family activity.

When it comes to holidays, Christmas is the biggest. The kids moan and laugh about how many decorations I've accumulated over the years, but once again, I'm working on a theme! I like to have the house decorated by December 1st so we can celebrate the holiday for the entire month. I want to concentrate on being fully grateful for our time together and all that we have.

We entertain a lot during the holidays, and we donate time at a homeless shelter named Second Harvest. On Christmas Eve or Christmas morning, we go to mass. This is a big part of the celebration as well. These various activities result in a lot of family bonding throughout December.

When the kids were little, Phil and I would wait for Christmas Eve to tackle gifts labeled "some assembly required" and dig in to help Santa. We'd end up spending the early hours of Christmas morning assembling. These assembly marathons were a bonding experience for Phil and me. By dawn, we were exhausted, and then the children would wake up. They were up and excited. Their glee was worth every minute of lost sleep, and Santa always came through, even if a few extra bolts or washers hadn't found the right home.

I wanted Spencer and Jacqueline to experience some Santa Claus magic in their youngest years, so I took Christmas Eve even one step further. I'd send Phil up to the roof when it was time for the kids to go to bed on Christmas Eve. Phil would make loud noises, and I would say, "Oh my, it's the reindeer! The reindeer are here. The reindeer. Oh my God. Santa's going to know you're awake. Santa won't stop here if he knows you're awake."

After a quick scurry, Spencer and Jacqueline would be in bed and asleep, seemingly within seconds. We'd leave cookies and milk out for Santa as well as carrots outside for the reindeer. We made a lot of excitement—a lot of buildup to the big event on Christmas morning.

Now that the kids are older, I enjoy giving "experiences" over "things." One of James's favorite gifts was when I arranged for Phil to go on a special fishing trip with his two sons, James and Spencer. I have learned that people often forget the material gift of a sweater, perfume, or shoes—but we all remember unique experiences. The experiences don't need to be expensive, simply highly personalized, matching the person's unique interests. When someone takes the time to design an experience that "fits" you perfectly, you remember.

While I love Christmas and everything it stands for, I don't feel the same about New Year's Eve. In fact, in our home, we have altered the focus of this holiday. After the hype and excitement of Christmas, we gather as a large family—all four children and their spouses—around the dinner table on New Year's Eve. The tradition, which started as an hour-long dinner, has evolved into a whole evening around the table.

We reflect and talk about what we feel good and proud about over the last 12 months. We identify our biggest accomplishments and think about how these accomplishments make us feel. Then we identify our "do-overs," talking about where we screwed up and what we wish we had handled differently. In other words, we ask ourselves: What went well? What could we do better the next time?

We each ask ourselves some hard questions:

- In situations where I have screwed up, have I apologized to the person(s) or involved?

- Does the person know that I'd love to have a big do-over for the situation?

- Have I had the conversations I need to have?

- Do I need to apologize for something?

- Do I need to forgive someone?

We share our answers as a family and then, if the situation involves other people, we encourage each other to take that next step. It's one thing to recognize your mistakes; it's another thing to take that next step and make amends if you need to.

Once we've completed our time of reflection, it's time to discuss and score the New Year's resolutions we made the previous year. Let me explain: By Jan 15th of each year, every member of our family writes down 10 New Year's resolutions, plus a bonus one. The resolutions need to be the person's goals for the year, and they must be as quantifiable as possible. For example, one year a goal was to run 12 5k races the following year, one each month.

On New Year's Eve, we pull out the goals, report on how we did, and get our scores. As with everything else in our family, it's a big competition.

You get 10 points for every resolution you achieved; 5 points if you made a concentrated effort and got 50% there; and 0 points if you got less than 50% there. The person with the highest score gets bragging rights and his or her name and year on the family trophy—a fist pump with names and years of the winners posted.

Spencer takes on the role of reading new resolutions aloud to make sure they're quantifiable enough. You don't get points in this competition if your resolutions are not quantifiable. For example, when Shannon says, "I want more date nights with my husband," Spencer asks, "What does that mean and how many more date nights?"

We take the resolutions seriously because they are important to each of us and because they allow us to continue to improve. We identify our goals and areas in which we simply want to get better. We share these goals and vulnerabilities with the entire family. The completion just makes it more like a game!

We learn a great deal about each other, and we have the information needed to support each other in meaningful ways through the year. We sometimes push each other on things we know are important. Who doesn't need someone to lovingly check in and provide a gentle nudge or a direct push?

* * * * *

Every family is different, and the best approach for your family's holidays, vacations, and birthdays will be unique to your family. What's common to us all is the need to disconnect from the everyday and hold these times sacred. No matter how busy or important your job, give yourself and your family the gift of full-out time together. The bonds you create and the memories you share will last a lifetime.

Celebrations and vacations are, by nature, intentional times; they are bright spots breaking up our busy, everyday lives. In the hectic nature of our workaday world, we can only be intentional about so many things at home. Sometimes, we just have to get through the day as best we can.

I've come to realize that even during our non-intentional moments, kids of working moms are often learning skills that give them an advantage over other kids.

KEY TAKEAWAYS

- **WHILE FLEXIBILITY IS GENERALLY A GOOD THING, CERTAIN TIMES MUST BE SACRED FOR FAMILY**
  Typically, families with working moms need to be flexible about routines and accept that work will

sometimes spill over into family time. But vacation and celebration times are another story altogether. You need to fully engage with the family during these bonding times. Get away from normal distractions and turn all devices off to the extent that you can. While this may seem impossible, given today's expectations, you must make the effort, even if only during certain times of the day, especially dinner. If you get a week or two weeks away with your family each year, make every minute available to you a quality minute.

- **THOUGHTFUL CELEBRATIONS SEND POWERFUL MESSAGES OF LOVE**
  The power of celebrations is more about the intention and attention you put into them than the money involved. The guest of honor must feel loved, appreciated, and celebrated—not as if no expense has been spared, but that so much thoughtfulness is behind the celebration. For example, you can have as much fun in a public park as you can at a fancy venue.

- **HOLIDAYS ARE FOR BONDING**
  Holidays provide opportunities to bond in a variety of ways: be together, be grateful, serve others, and reflect upon how things are going in life. And a friendly competition never hurts.

- **CONVERSATION, REFLECTION, ENCOURAGEMENT—AND EVEN ACCOUNTABILITY MATTER**
  As you plan the various special times your family spends together, be sure to include time for conversation, reflection, encouragement—and even accountability. The best relationships include love, laughter, and depth.

CHAPTER 6

KIDS ARE ALWAYS LEARNING: THE M&M DISASTER

ONE DAY DURING SPENCER'S FIRST YEAR IN COLLEGE, I got a call from my frustrated son. He was pledging a fraternity and had been involved in planning a mixer. He had called to tell me the story behind his frustration.

The fraternity had assembled a planning meeting in which individuals were assigned responsibilities for food, drinks, setting up the room, etc. Someone suggested putting M&Ms at the table near the entrance and took responsibility for the task.

When Spencer arrived at the event, he was shocked. A bowl at the entrance of the event held regular, grocery-store variety M&Ms. "Mom," he said, "I was expecting the scarlet red and gold colors of our fraternity, but they just went and bought M&Ms. It's like I don't even know what they are doing. Performance is not at a high level."

I laugh every time I remember this story because it's a perfect example of how our kids absorb lessons from us— some intentional and many unintentional.

Spencer assumed the fraternity would get M&Ms the color of the fraternity, if not ones with the actual Greek letters on them, because that's what I would have done. I always go over the top for these sorts of things. As I explained in the last chapter, I'm convinced celebrations are important; I enjoy planning a fun event; and my time at Disney made me a bit of a theme junkie.

None of this means I believe that a fraternity or any other party will fail if someone happens to buy the wrong color M&Ms—and I'm certain I never suggested such a thing to my kids.

I'm skilled at and enjoy planning and executing full-out themed parties. (I guess that aspect of Disney is now part of my DNA.) Spencer and Jaqueline watched and participated in the process throughout their lives, and now they *own* the skill. Perhaps their expectations of a good party could benefit from a bit of adjustment, especially if someone else is hosting—but nothing changes the fact that they own the skill of putting together a well-themed party.

Kids of working moms can be expected to absorb the skills of planning, prioritizing, and problem solving because the mom naturally demonstrates those professional skills at home as well as at work. Working moms demonstrate professional skills on a daily, weekly, and monthly basis, often without being aware of it.

I remember a time when Spencer was exposed to the habit of continual improvement. Spencer was 11 years old when we moved from Florida to California in July, a month earlier than originally planned. With the earlier date came a logistical challenge.

Each summer, we allowed the kids to pick one or two camps to attend. That year, Spencer had chosen a basketball camp at Duke University. He was signed up, paid in full, and ready to go.

From Florida, we had anticipated that we would put Spencer on a direct flight to North Carolina, and then friends who also had a son attending the camp would pick him up at the airport. From California, things were more complicated, because the trip would involve a transfer in Chicago.

Spencer really wanted to attend this camp, and he was willing to learn how to navigate on his own, so we decided to let him go—but not without doing everything possible to ensure his safety.

We took Spencer to the airport and practiced. He learned to read a ticket, identify the proper gate number, identify the time for boarding, follow signs to the gate, and wait until it was time to board. I remember showing him how to do this and then quietly walking beside Spencer as he figured it out for himself. We practiced until we were all confident that Spencer had the skills he needed to get to North Carolina.

For the flight out, we walked with Spencer to the gate, and, with cell phone in hand (but more like a flip phone than a smartphone back then), our son got on the plane. The transfer went without a hitch, and our friends picked Spencer up at the airport. The return flight, however, wasn't so smooth.

I got a call from Spencer, already in Chicago, telling me that something was wrong. His plane from Chicago to California wasn't ready and he was unsure of what was happening. Because there was no flight, no one seemed to be in charge of Spencer. In fact, a flight attendant had taken him to what seemed like an air traffic controller's station and left him. While Spencer was excited to see people moving what looked like Lego planes around, he was also scared. He was alone in Chicago and didn't know how he would get home.

Panic rose in my chest as I realized we had neglected to plan for such a scenario. My son might find himself overnight in Chicago without an adult to help him. How had I let this happen? You can imagine how I was beating myself up inside.

As long as I was on the phone with him, Spencer wasn't completely panicking. I was—and I was running names in my personal and professional network through my brain, looking for someone near Chicago. I couldn't believe Phil and I hadn't thought this cross-country trip completely through.

Things were dicey for a couple of hours until a flight attendant retrieved Spencer, his plane took off, and I could breathe again.

Getting off the plane, Spencer was so excited that he had managed on his own. This was a major accomplishment, and Spencer felt on top of the world.

During the car ride home, I said, "Let's talk about what went well, and what we might do differently next time." I told Spencer that Mommy hadn't done it right, and that I'd learned something important from the experience.

Looking back, I realize that I naturally evaluated the situation and learned from it. It didn't occur to me to avoid letting Spencer know I had made a mistake or that both of us could use a process to learn from this scary experience. I encouraged continual improvement at home as well as at work. Because this has been our family habit, Spencer and Jaqueline own this process too.

Spencer's plane trip across the country at age 11 stands on its own as an example—perhaps an extreme one—of the sense of independence my kids had growing up. In general, we encouraged independence while practicing and preparing the kids for success. This was intentional.

On the other hand, my kids needed to do some things on their own simply because I didn't have time to do those things for them. For example, Jacqueline became the go-to girl for French braids for her entire lacrosse team.

As a child, she wanted her hair braided, but I could never figure out how to do it. So, Jacqueline taught herself and can braid her own hair and that of her entire team. We still laugh about this. I don't laugh quite as hard about picture day because I have some regrets over that.

It seemed that, for one reason or another, I was always out of town for school pictures day. The wall going into my bedroom displays a picture of each child for each year of his or her life. It also demonstrates my absence on picture days.

Since I wasn't home on the appropriate days and picking out outfits isn't Phil's strong suit, Jacqueline's 5th and 6th grade pictures feature the exact same shirt, only in a different color. And it was like a tee shirt. Jaqueline liked the shirt, but it wasn't the most flattering one she owned.

When I walk by that wall, I sometimes feel bad, but I am also reminded that I am probably the only person who cares. Jaqueline loved her school pictures each year.

As a mom, I have always been determined to be available for the important times in my kids' lives, the joyful moments as well as the moments of crisis. I was deliberate about being home between 5 p.m. and 8 p.m. when the kids were little, and I made sure the kids had access to me when needed during work hours. I attended their important games, even if I had to sometimes step away to take a call. Fostering independence has nothing to do with neglect.

Even so, being available for important moments in our kids' lives is not the same as being available for every moment. Being available for every moment can clip our children's wings and prevent or delay maturity. Ask any college administrator how he or she feels about helicopter parenting.

Finding the right moments to be available is a dynamic exercise. Working moms must hone and rely on the skills that make them good professionals at home as well as at work. These skills include planning, prioritizing, organizing, delegating, and problem solving.

I am convinced that demonstration of these skills in the homes of working moms gives their children a unique advantage. Of course, all moms must manage time and resources, but the need for these skills is typically elevated for working moms. And working moms automatically bring the professional skills they practice during work hours home with them.

There's no doubt the professional training and experiences I've had at work make me a better person and mom as well as a better professional. I have access to feedback and resources that equip me to be a better manager of time and challenging situations, wherever I happen to be. I also have many opportunities to make mistakes and learn from them—and I do both routinely.

Kids who see their parents regularly demonstrate planning, prioritizing, and problem-solving skills absorb these skills, often without either the kids or parents noticing it happening. For example, when I asked Spencer to think about what went well as well as what might be improved on his plane trip, I was using a critical thinking process we use at work all the time.

After a project is completed, we look at what worked and what we can learn for the next project. I naturally involve Spencer and Jacqueline in this process after events in our lives—whether those events are vacations, parties, or school projects. We routinely reinforce what we've done well and seek to improve. On most occasions, I'm not even fully aware that I'm transferring a process we use at work to my parenting. I'm not lecturing; I'm just doing what I do. Spencer and Jacqueline aren't consciously learning; they are absorbing.

* * * * *

For a professional mom, prioritizing means some things get let go and some things get left to the child who wants them. In my house, meticulously organized closets got left until another season in life, and braiding hair got left to the daughter who wanted braided hair. I don't feel guilty on either account. Multiplying these examples by countless day-to-day decisions has resulted in both Jacqueline and Spencer becoming critical thinking and independent young adults. I'm immensely proud of them, and I believe my role as a working mom was an important contribution.

Here is the point I especially want to emphasize: As I talk to Spencer and Jacqueline as young adults, they reveal skills and ways of thinking that they *absorbed*—skills I was not consciously teaching even as my kids were integrating them into their lives. Spencer's experience with the M&Ms at his fraternity event is an example. While I was simply planning parties for my family and friends, Spencer was learning about *branding* and *congruency*. How amazing is that? When your guilt about being a working mom rears its ugly head, tell it *that* story.

I remember a phone call I got from Jacqueline during her first year at college. "Mom," she said, "the parents of my friends still do everything for them. My roommate told me she needs her mom to get her prescription. I told her to get it herself. She complained that she doesn't know how. Who doesn't know how to go to CVS and pick up a prescription?"

Incidents such as these shocked Jacqueline, who, as a college freshman, felt able to accomplish pretty much anything on her own. My daughter admits that as she was growing up, she sometimes resented that her parents' worlds didn't revolve solely around her, and that if she wanted certain things to happen, she'd have to figure them out on her own. As a young adult, Jacqueline is grateful, appreciating the value of independence and the ability to figure things out.

On a big scale, Jacqueline chose her major and career path based on her fascination with my job, which I shared with both kids throughout their lives. From their teddy bear boss game, to daily conversations about each of our days, to the times we entertained for business, my job was integrated into our lives as a family.

On a smaller scale, Jaqueline believes she learned the skill of planning from me, almost by osmosis. The skills I developed in planning and managing IT projects at work were always in play while planning the parties and vacations that were a hallmark of our family's experience together. Sometimes these were big events that required juggling diverse schedules and interests. While my children laugh at my color-coded itineraries, they understand the value in them.

Today, Spencer understands the value of branding, and Jacqueline has confidence that she can plan any event or trip she desires. Recently, she was proud of a weekend she planned just days before she, her father and I left. She found some reward miles and figured out how to purchase only one round-trip ticket for the three of us to travel in six days. She says, "This is something you would have figured out, Mom. I just learned along the way."

Spencer believes that both he and Jacqueline have learned to express themselves, present an argument, and say what's on their minds because they've seen me model these professional skills repeatedly. My kids learned that when they need something, it's their job to speak up—and not to wait around for others to speak on their behalf.

Spencer says, "Seeing how you handle yourself taught us that if there is something important, we have to stand up for it. We say what we have to say. That's a big thing we learned from you."

From my perspective, one of the biggest learnings I could share with my kids came from the experience of traveling. I've never understood why schools strongly disapprove of kids going on trips with their families during the school year. That time of family bonding, as well as the lessons kids absorb simply by being in different environments, is priceless.

Family trips were times when Phil and I demonstrated the priority of family. We demonstrated how to leave work behind and immerse ourselves into what we were doing together. As with most things, the value and learning involved didn't depend on elaborate expenditures, although we were fortunate to have the means to travel internationally sometimes.

You can learn a great deal from museums and historic places in your own or a nearby city, north or south. The activities of setting aside time, choosing activities, budgeting resources, and experiencing different people and perspectives build skills and open minds in young and old alike.

Spencer learned about exchange rates and the value of the U.S. dollar with a memorable experience on our first international trip as a family. Selfishly, I never wanted my kids to nickel and dime me on vacations, constantly asking for money for souvenirs or activities. To eliminate this annoyance, I had the kids do chores for money before each trip. They earned their own vacation money.

The kids had a set amount of money they could spend however they wanted to on any given trip. It was their responsibility to manage their spending according to their own priorities. This taught them budget responsibility as well as the tough process of making hard choices. They could choose to spend money on themselves or buy small presents for their friends.

On this particular trip, we almost had a breakdown. Spencer had $100 to spend on our international cruise. As we were unpacking in the room, he went to the ATM to exchange his U.S. dollars into euro currency. A few minutes later, Spencer came bursting into the room, enraged. And distraught. He had lost $18 in the exchange and felt that his own money had been stolen from him.

Spencer was so angry that he refused to spend a dime on that entire vacation. On the other hand, we had a discussion about international currency and the strength of the U.S. dollar that Spencer has never forgotten. No lecture or textbook could have imparted such powerful learning.

At whatever level a family can afford, traveling imparts lessons in geography, history, and culture as well as the skills of planning, organizing, and budgeting.

Kids naturally learn from their family routines, processes, and experiences. Some of these lessons, such as Spencer's lesson on international currency, happen within obvious, if not always intentional ways. Others, such as Spencer's approach to party planning, happen without anyone noticing. This "absorption" is constantly happening.

If I could accomplish only one thing with this book, it would be to dispel the myth that working moms cheat their children. Working moms aren't ruining their children, and they needn't feel guilty about their career choices. When guilt strikes, working moms should fight back with the knowledge that kids absorb the skills, strengths, and patterns they see demonstrated in their parents. Successful working moms, by definition, must build strengths in the areas of prioritizing, delegating, planning, and communicating. These are life skills they naturally bring home and impart to their children. The next time you feel guilty about your store-bought cookies or your deficient skills in hair braiding, keep this bigger picture in mind.

KEY TAKEAWAYS

- **KIDS OF WORKING MOMS GAIN ADVANTAGE IN INDEPENDENCE**
  Assuming that parents are consistently available for the important things in their lives, children of working moms naturally learn a degree of independence during the moments their parents are at work. Being available for every moment is helicopter parenting. It can clip a child's wings and prevent or delay maturity.

- **CHILDREN ARE LIKE SPONGES—THIS IS A GOOD THING**
  In addition to the lessons they learn from the deliberate instruction of their parents, children automatically absorb thought and behavior patterns they see demonstrated on a regular basis. This reality provides distinct advantages to kids of working moms. While all moms have to plan, prioritize, and problem solve, the need for these skills is typically elevated for working moms.

- **PROFESSIONAL MOMS PASS ON PROFESSIONAL SKILLS TO THEIR KIDS, INTENTIONALLY AND UNINTENTIONALLY**
  Professional moms have access to feedback and resources that equip them to be competent managers of time and challenging situations. These resources enrich their home lives and are passed down seamlessly to their children. For example, a working mom may engage her children in

performance evaluation and improvement processes without even thinking about it. The children not only grow up to understand the process without effort, but they can also work through the process when they need it.

CHAPTER 7

KEEPING CONNECTED:
CAR TALK AND RESPECTFUL STALKING

HAVE YOU NOTICED how the best parenting insights and opportunities can come unbidden and out of nowhere? Sometimes in the midst of our busy working and parenting days, life simply gives us a gift. Phil and I received such a gift one day while on a road trip. I recognized the gift when I saw it, grabbed ahold, and held on for all I was worth.

Spencer was in seventh grade at the time, with Jaqueline two years behind. We were all in the car motoring along, having a normal conversation, when Spencer asked a question about sex. Phil and I barely glanced at each other before I answered the question as directly and honestly as I could.

Since the topic had been raised, I asked the kids, "What other questions do you have?" Spencer began rattling things off—his questions, his confusion, the misinformation he was getting from his friends, extended family, television, or Internet. And we talked for 30–40 minutes before we reached our destination.

There was something magic about this conversation, and I could tell that a window had opened in which Spencer felt safe asking his questions. It was wonderful to learn what he was thinking and struggling with, and to have this conversation in *his* timing rather than ours.

Being in the car, where Phil and I were facing forward, rather than looking directly at the kid's eyeball-to-eyeball, lessened the awkwardness inherent in the topic and drained some of the intensity. It became a "casual conversation," with Phil and I both trying to answer the questions as directly as we could while not being overly dramatic.

During the same conversation, Jacqueline blurted out that she liked a boy at school. Spencer began to tease her a bit and then it hit me … the car had become a "safe zone," a place where we could talk about anything without judgment, fear, or feeling stupid. We needed to "package this" and claim it as our sanctioned place of unfiltered safety and privacy.

That day, we christened the dynamic that had emerged as *car talk* and made it an official family practice. The rules of car talk are threefold:

1. In the car, no subject is off limits
   You can ask anything you want or talk about any problem. You can even experiment with saying things we wouldn't tolerate in other venues.

2. In the car, there's no judgment
   There are no dumb questions and no put-downs.

3. What is said in the car, stays in the car
   Only the people in the car are party to the conversation, and once you get out of the car, the conversation is over. No one is ever allowed to divulge the confidentially of the discussion or elements of the discussion.

The car became a sanctuary where the kids could be their most awkward or curious selves. It's not that Phil or I were in the habit of judging the kids or putting them down, it's just that the car became its own special entity. Conversations in the car had a unique feel and depth to them. Spencer says:

> I learned about drugs and alcohol. I learned about sex and where a baby comes from. The car was a place where I distinctly remember some learning curves as a young kid. Then my questions and concerns started escalating in high school and college where alcohol and drugs were readily available, and my friends were drinking. I was an athlete who would get in trouble for drinking. What was I supposed to do in those situations? I didn't want to rat anyone out, but I didn't want to go to the parties, either. When I didn't know what to do, I'd ask my parents for guidance when we were in the car. I could have conversations I wouldn't be comfortable having in other places.

Open communication is the lifeblood of every healthy family, and I worked hard to make sure this was a characteristic of our little group. I wanted to be sure that I knew what was going on in the kids' lives at every age, at least as best as a parent could. I wasn't perfect at this, not by a long shot, but I tried to put routines in place to encourage openness. Car talk was one of our best practices, and I can't even take credit for it. It began as a spontaneous thing.

When the kids were little, as you know, that time between 5 p.m. and 8 p.m. was sacred, and I did a lot of listening as well as playing and reading books aloud during those hours. Phil and I always asked about Spencer and Jaqueline's days and tried to listen patiently to their answers. Most nights, we ate dinner as a family, playing the roses and thorns game I had learned from my friend.

From their youngest ages, Phil and I treated the kids' days as important as we treated our own. I believe that when kids feel respected, they are likely to be open about what they think and feel. I also believe it helps kids to know that adults have bad days and struggles too.

I was also careful to ask the kids about their experiences with caregivers and teachers. We didn't have a nanny camera, but I certainly wanted to know what the kids were feeling and observing about their caregivers. With the information they gave, we found it necessary to make several corrections before we got the right nanny.

The post-project questions I brought home from work helped us debrief Spencer's solo trip across the country at age 11, as well as many other experiences. These questions were routine for us, helping us to examine and communicate after family projects or initiatives. We routinely debriefed by asking, "What went well?" and "What can we do better next time?" If one member of the family's priorities weren't met or feelings were hurt, we talked about what had happened and made plans to do better the next time. I think this fostered vulnerability while building the mindset of continuous improvement.

Being together, having fun, celebrating special occasions, and vacationing together all create bonds that foster communication. But none of that means a family can escape the struggles inherent in raising adolescents. Spencer and Jacqueline were normal kids with the immaturity and struggles that come with it. As they navigated those confusing and critical years, I knew I needed to be attuned to what was happening in their lives, even as the kids were fighting for independence.

At the same time, I'm convinced our children have a right to privacy, just as we do. My mother didn't read my diary when I was growing up. She respected my diary as a special place to put my private thoughts. She trusted me, and that meant a lot to me. I followed her lead with my own kids.

I look at the social media world, at least to some extent, as *their* space. I wasn't willing to ruin our trust by having parental controls that monitor each click and every keystroke and then question the kids about it. I didn't want to spy on them and use GPSs and other monitoring tools.

As CIO of Symantec, it is critical to recognize that we have made great advancements in the technology that allows you to monitor and have parental control in age-appropriate ways. I absolutely turn them on when my grandchildren now come and visit. But when Spencer and Jacqueline were in those early teenage years, I emphasized trust. I expected the truth from them and vice versa. I would not tolerate anything else.

From my view, if you can't have an open conversation, with trust, you have a problem. It all comes down to trust. I needed to trust my children, and they needed to trust Phil and me. Both Spencer and Jacqueline knew that if they lied to us, they would face severe consequences.

Even as I trusted the kids, I asked to become Facebook friends to both Spencer and Jacqueline. The entire social media phenomenon was new and surrounded with uncertainty. As a friend on Facebook, I could sort of watch and see what was going on behind the scenes. I did not, however, add comments. If a parent adds comments, kids respond, "Oh my God. You're stalking me." They are embarrassed in front of their friends.

Because I didn't make comments, sometimes the kids, especially Jacqueline, forgot that I was sort of watching. And one day I recognized a dynamic from my own generation. During the years that girls are in roughly sixth through eighth grade, mean girls and groups of mean girls emerge.

Plenty of literature exists about this phenomenon and the reasons behind it; I am simply aware of how important it is for parents of young teenage girls to pay close attention to what's happening. Know your daughter's friends and who she hangs out with. These years, when girls are so vulnerable, and their self-worth is determined only by their "friends," can be a very destructive period.

When I went to school, this stuff happened, but by the time three o'clock rolled around, you got outside the school walls, went and played sports, or did something else. The next morning, the petty things that went on the day before were forgotten and we were on to the next item. For this generation, because of social media, the petty stuff continues on and on, sometimes all night long, and its reach gets broader and broader, with many who were not even involved in the incident weighing in.

What might have started as a disagreement between two girls now has 30 people giving opinions on it, and it just doesn't stop. And often one of the two girls is taking the brunt of the battle.

(In general, people weigh in on social media because they have an opinion and want to ensure their voice is heard. I think it's fantastic to get all opinions and views out into the open to debate and discuss. What bothers me is that the debate and conversation has become so charged with emotion, and often rage. Being hidden behind our keyboard can, in some cases, make us feel more courageous. Here is a question that is worth exploring in a future book: Is social media making us better or worse human beings? Provocative, right?)

Sometimes, when Jaqueline was in her room, I would peek in and ask about her and her day. She'd respond by saying that nothing was wrong or that she didn't want to talk about it. As a mother, I could tell something was wrong.

On those days, I would go on Facebook and find out what was going on. I could often see that some conflict was happening, even if I couldn't fully understand it from the posts.

This was my cue to casually suggest we run an errand or get some ice cream. Getting Jaqueline in the car often allowed me to help her through the situation without me acknowledging that I knew it was going on. Car talk allowed her to feel safe and open up without feeling interrogated by me.

This painful stuff is going to happen—none of us escapes it. For a parent, it's important to figure out what's happening, change the environment, and help your kids redirect and refocus—all without them feeling you're being intrusive or failing to trust them. For me, both checking in on Facebook and orchestrating car talk by going on a ride for some purpose really worked.

Getting kids to communicate about what is going on with their friends is delicate, even in the car, and I did my best to be subtle. I'd ask, "How is Sally doing, anyway? What's going on with her?" Over time, the problem might come out, and we could talk in the no-judgment sanctuary of the car.

I also tried to protect my relationships with the kids by picking my battles, knowing that kids don't open up to parents when they are angry at those same parents. There were years when my relationship with Jaqueline wasn't easy, especially those years between 13 and 15. I couldn't understand her mood swings or figure out what to do with them. Sometimes I would phone her on my way home from work and joke, saying, "I'm coming home, and I want to know if I'm going to get the Jacqueline who likes me or the one who hates me. Which one am I getting today?"

Most days this made us chuckle and move through the issues quickly. But let's be real: The mother/daughter relationship during those couple of years is tough. Plenty of books are written about these years and how to cope with them. I confirm what many others told me: This temporary alien that daughters turn into (yes, they all do) does return to be a wonderful, caring, mature, loving person. Jacqueline and I are on the other side now, and I can proudly say she is one of my best friends.

Another critical aspect of parenting that can be especially tough for working moms to carry out is discipline. My mother always told me that discipline is a form of love. While Mom was right, the last thing working moms want to do when we get home is discipline our children. More than anything, we want to spend time with our kids, creating memories. We want to hug them and make sure they know how deeply they are loved. Yet, on some days when we walk in the door at the end of the day, these warm expressions are not what our children need.

When the kids were younger, I found the "time-out" chair effective. When they did something wrong, terrorized their sibling, or acted outright disrespectful, we had them sit in the time-out chair, which faced the wall. They had to remove themselves from play or the activity in the room and sit in that chair.

Most experts who advocate this method recommend time-out should last one minute per age of the child. In other words, when a kid is three years old, his or her time out lasts three minutes. That's a long time for a three-year-old to be quiet and disengaged from the family—but it effectively removes them from the attention they are often seeking from acting out. It also gives them needed time to calm down.

In our house, the time-out period ended with the offending child needing to apologize in whatever way was appropriate. I would also ask the child if he or she understood why the behavior in question was unacceptable. This was really hard, when all I wanted was to enjoy those beautiful kids and keep the peace. I did discipline the kids because I came to realize that if Phil and I didn't, nobody would. It was our responsibility.

As with all aspects of our home, I wanted to be fair in discipline, and I wanted the rules to apply to everyone, even Phil and me. I would occasionally put myself in time-out, if, for example, I broke a promise to the kids.

As they got older, Spencer and Jacqueline loved putting me in time-out, but they also felt bad about it. They always wanted to let me out early. While the minute-per-year didn't apply to me, I wanted the kids to know that all of us, including me, are accountable for our behavior.

As the kids get older, they need discipline just as much, but the style needs to change, to get a bit harsher. When something truly important is at stake, such as trust, I want to come down unequivocally, so the message is remembered for a long time.

When Jacqueline was 16 years old, we bought her an old car. On the first day she got her license, Jacqueline drove her friend to the movies. It is against the law in our state for 16-year-olds to drive their peers for the first year they are licensed. Sixteen-year-olds can only drive themselves or siblings.

I discovered mid-movie that Jacqueline had broken this law and our rules. I contacted her by phone, asking where she was and how she had gotten there. She claimed that her friend's mother had driven the girls, dropping them off at the theater. When I asked for the mother's phone number, so I could confirm this story (a mother always knows), Jacqueline was forced to confess to driving herself and her friend to the movies.

I insisted Jacqueline come home immediately, and she lost car privileges for weeks. She had her license and her own car, which sat in the driveway unused for several weeks.

I needed to send the message that driving is a privilege, not a right. I expect my kids to behave within the parameters of the law and, perhaps more important, to tell me the truth. If our relationship is built upon lies, I can't trust my kids. As I recall, this was the only time she lied so blatantly. The punishment was severe, but it needed to teach a clear lesson.

* * * * *

While my relationships with Shannon and James are naturally different from the ones I have with Spencer and Jaqueline, bonding and open communication is a priority in my relationships with them as well. When Shannon and James were younger and we lived in different states, I put effort into making sure they were included in holidays and vacations. Shannon, thankfully, remembers me as being welcoming from the beginning of our relationship.

While James might echo that, he is prone to remember his impression of me the first time we met—seeing his dad pull up in a convertible with a much younger blonde!

Both Shannon and James were in our wedding and visited us for vacations in Florida. I put my love of planning to work in organizing outings and trips to make their visits with us special. Shannon still loves the birthstone ring we gave her for her 13th birthday.

Shannon, a working mother of two, considers me a role model of a professional working mom for her. I relish that role. For both Shannon and James, I am a sounding board for career-related issues. We have many talks about ambition and strategies for handling certain situations. We also talk about personal challenges and methods to solve them.

One time, after their mother had died, Shannon and James weren't getting along. Unfortunately, they had to deal with the death of their mother at a young age and had to make a ton of adult decisions before they were ready or should have needed to. Shannon and James are very different and didn't always agree on the appropriate path forward. I could see and feel the relationship between the two of them growing contentious and unhealthy.

Given our values surrounding the importance of family, I told them both that the next time we got together, we were going to talk through the issues and get everything on the table. They would work out their differences and then bury the hatchet. That's what we did—at least sort of.

One weekend when we were together for Spencer's college graduation, Phil, Shannon, James, and I found a quiet place to have breakfast. Phil and I facilitated the discussion, and I transcribed all the important things that were said. Together, we clarified what Shannon and James needed from each other; what annoyed each of them; what aspects of this tragic experience they wished were different; and more important, how they would get their relationship back on a positive track and move beyond it.

I thought it was important to symbolize that this conflict was in the past and would stay there. So, the next time we were together at our family cabin, I produced a sharp hatchet, as well as the notes I had taken about the past. The two of them again talked through differences and committed to keeping the conflict in the past and moving forward. When we went to bury the hatchet, however, the ground was frozen! We dug a bit harder (an ironic symbolism), and the hatchet and notes were buried. We indeed buried the hatchet!

Everyone was happy except for Phil, who thought I should have bought a rubber hatchet rather than a real one. I think he selfishly wanted to keep that nice, sharp hatchet!

I've tried to teach all my children that good communication, whether in a marriage, family, friendship, or workplace, is not automatic. Good communication takes time and intention. It takes the willingness to be direct and get things out in the open. It means speaking up and asking for what you need. Sometimes, good communication means admitting that you are wrong and asking for forgiveness. This is a discipline that needs to be built into your everyday life, especially with loved ones.

One of my favorite ways of building communication into our family life is our New Year's Eve dinner, which you've already read about. We give ourselves time for self-reflection and communicate our goals, our triumphs, and the things that didn't go so well. We encourage each other and hold each other accountable. At some points of the evening, we are somber, but at other points, we compete, laugh, and sometimes cry. Always, we leave the table with a stronger bond and greater knowledge of and respect for one another. We have a greater understanding of how we can help and support each other to be better!

KEY TAKEAWAYS

- **INTENTIONALLY CREATING SPECIAL SPACE FOR CONVERSATION KEEPS LINES OF COMMUNICATION OPEN**
  Creating special "space" for your kids to ask questions and say what's on their minds can help your family achieve open communication. In our family, we used the car as a sanctuary for awkward or difficult conversations. We found that talking with the parents facing forward, rather

than eyeball-to-eyeball with the kids, reduced awkwardness. We also had a rule that anything said in the car stayed in the car. It couldn't come back to haunt the kids later.

- **HABITS OF LISTENING REGULARLY TO CHILDREN BUILDS SKILLS AND SELF-ESTEEM**
  Listening to children and asking about both the good and bad in their days creates a foundation of sharing and mutual respect. Doing this from the youngest ages builds confidence as well as the ability and willingness to express ideas and opinions.

- **WHILE KIDS DON'T RESPOND WELL TO SPYING, YOU NEED TO BE ALERT**
  Kids don't respond well if they think you are spying on them, but you still need to be attuned to what's going on in their lives. Being friends on Facebook—without making comments—can help you get a good idea of their friends and their issues. Good technology tools can help you appropriately use parental controls and keep your kids safe.

- **VULNERABILITY FOSTERS TRUST**
  Two elements that foster open communication are being vulnerable about your own challenges and letting your kids know you trust them and respect their privacy.

- **UNDERSTAND DISCIPLINE AS A FORM OF LOVE**
  At the end of a long workday, a mom wants nothing more than to embrace, enjoy, and celebrate her children. The last thing she wants to do is discipline. The fact that discipline is hard doesn't make it less than important. Providing boundaries and holding family members accountable to those boundaries is every parent's responsibility.

CHAPTER 8

ONE JOB COMPLEMENTS ANOTHER: FOR BETTER AND BETTER

O N THE SURFACE, it seems the job I have as Chief Mom couldn't be more different from my job as Chief Information Officer for a corporation. It would seem—and to me it often *has* seemed—like the two roles play tug of war with each other, with the only product being a heavy load of guilt.

With hindsight being 20/20, I'm confident this surface view is wrong. Rather than steal time and attention from each other, each of my primary jobs makes me better at the other— as well as a better person overall.

For starters, there's nothing like a full plate of responsibility to build your skills in multitasking. When I became a parent, I was struck anew by how limited and precious time is. My ever-present goal, both at home and at work, is to optimize the hours I have. Since I don't have unlimited time in either place, I must constantly prioritize and reprioritize. As a new mom, I came to quickly realize that minutes matter.

In the face of our cultural model of the perfect family and spotless house, I didn't find it easy to give myself permission to let some things go. I didn't find it easy to release some tendencies toward perfectionism or accept that others who don't share my priorities might (would) criticize me.

Carrying guilt that stems from other people's standards is neither necessary nor healthy. Eventually, I learned to laugh rather than beat myself up. Letting go of the guilt truly freed me to enjoy life more.

I've come to understand that anyone can be busy at any job for countless hours, especially in the high-tech world where change is constant. But activity doesn't equal importance. My goal is to use the hours at my disposal to deliver the biggest impact possible. I don't want to be busy; I want to produce results. I want to have an impact.

On Sunday nights, I review my calendar for the week, with the intent of discovering what I can let go, what I can shed. For example, if several IT professionals will be in a meeting, I typically don't need to be there as well. I can be more productive somewhere else.

Letting things go not only frees me up to deliver different results, it opens the door for others to develop and increase their responsibility. As a leader, a big part of my job is helping others grow and develop. Often, that means providing some coaching and then getting out of the way.

Whether I'm at home or at work, I practice being present, fully in the moment. If I am talking to one of the kids, he or she deserves my full attention. When Spencer and Jacqueline were little, I learned that I could help them with their homework or bake cookies, but not both at the same time. I could read them a story or fold laundry, but not at the same time. If I was distracted by housework or anything job related, my kids did not have my undivided attention. We could be in the same room and yet not be connecting or enjoying each other. Worse yet, my kids might feel rejected or as though they were not as important as this other thing.

When the kids were in one elementary school in Florida, I had morning carpool duties while my friend, Kaki Lucas, had the afternoon duties. I considered that 40-minute morning drive my special time with the kids. I was deliberate about using that time intentionally. We'd laugh, play games, call in to radio contests, talk about things that were important to the kids, and more. I built a strong, trusting relationship with each of the kids in the car. When I happened to be the parent who picked the kids up on 9/11, it was natural to have a conversation on their level about what it meant.

* * * * *

My friends always laughed at how I showed up at our children's sports events. I was the one wearing team colors, carrying pompoms and big foam fingers. My longtime friend Joanne Sykota still talks about how I used to bring a big Bose boom box and play "Who Let the Dogs Out" every time Spencer or Jacqueline scored a touchdown. (Yes, Jacqueline did play Pop Warner football for a few years. She will kill me for telling you.)

I showed up with the same enthusiasm at birthday parties, vacations, neighborhood 4th of July parties, and any number of friendly competitions. I still do. I am all in with everything I do. My dad instilled that in me, saying, "Why do anything if you are going to do it halfway [he actually said *half ass*]?"

The benefits of being all in are present in conversations with colleagues as well as with family and friends. I don't want to be thinking about what comes next. I want to be engaged on the issue at hand. That issue and that person deserve my full attention, just as my kids do.

Every Friday my team and I have a key critical IT initiative review, and I can get just as excited about site/standardization across the globe as I do ERP (Enterprise Resource Planning) consolidation, or even deleting legacy applications.

Each of these initiatives is both tactical and strategic in its own way, delivering an impact to the company in simplifying the IT, delivering cost savings, or making our employees more productive. Each requires and deserves my undivided attention.

Of course, life is constantly challenging and changing, and I don't mean to imply that any of us can always control distractions. As an IT professional, I had my phone with me at many of my kids' sporting events as I sought to integrate my work and life. I made it to the games, but if I needed to take a quick call, I could do that as well.

Here's my big point: We don't have to make the mistake of being our own distraction by doing multiple things in the same moment. In most situations, we can choose to let certain things go so that we can be all in, even if we can't be there as long as we might like. We don't have to be our own worst enemy.

* * * * *

Looking back on my career, I'm grateful that people believed in me and gave me opportunities, many of which I didn't recognize at the time. Some of the opportunities became seminal moments that altered my life and sent me along an unexpected path. While this isn't a book about work (that's the next book), I want to make one important point here to you as a working mom: You own your career.

Don't give ownership of your career away to an organization or manager. It's your career. Have a plan for your career and communicate your ambition and your aspirations—and keep your eyes open for something unexpected that might come your way.

Several times in my career, I was tapped on the shoulder to do something that I hadn't thought of. At times, a leader may see something in you that you don't see in yourself, especially during the early years of your career.

When someone offers you an opportunity, don't think of all the reasons you are not qualified and quickly say, "No." First, step back and think about it. Really think it over. I've had this sort of thing happen three times in my career. I wouldn't be a sitting Chief Information Officer if I hadn't taken those opportunities and run with them.

As a growing leader, I've received copious amounts of training, coaching, and feedback in my career. I've learned how to build a high-functioning team, deal with conflict productively, and make good decisions. Sometimes I was terrified, and sometimes I wasn't particularly grateful for all the feedback, but all of it has made me a better person, both as a leader and as a mother. We all say that feedback is a gift, and it really is.

When someone gives you feedback, it is because that person cares. Think about how hard it is for you to give feedback that draws attention to someone's need to improve. The words may not come out right, but you feel compelled or obligated to provide the truth to someone.

When someone makes the effort to give you feedback, assume positive intent. Assume that person is trying to make you better. Embrace feedback—I wish I had embraced it earlier in my career. Feedback is not pointing out a weakness; it is sharing an opportunity for growth.

I remember beginning my job at Cisco and discovering that the standards for presentations were far higher than the ones I had experienced at Disney. At Cisco, executives were constantly in presentation mode, often speaking at conferences to thousands rather than hundreds of people—without notes—on an enormous stage. It was lights, camera, action, and the executives were walking along the stage, in full animation, changing the volume of their voices to accentuate their points. I was terrified. I remember the sinking feeling as I thought, "I am petrified to speak. I am not very good at that."

I realized quickly that the job required me to be *great* at public speaking. I had to get comfortable, and fast. At first, I used my children and Phil as an audience. I would articulate the Cisco strategy by practicing on them.

After a couple of times, Spencer, Jacqueline, and Phil were eager to do their homework or essentially anything other than listening to me practice that same presentation again and again. Since I couldn't argue with that, I had to get creative.

We had just moved to California, and like all families that move, we had boxes we hadn't gotten to, and wouldn't get to for another year. I had a spare bedroom filled with boxes.

The spare bedroom became the meeting venue, and the kids' stuffed animals and dolls became my audience, sitting around on their boxes. I devoted one night a week to practicing presenting to an audience of stuffed animals in our guest bedroom.

During this process, I learned that I do much better with an interactive audience when I present. I like to see friendly faces, heads nodding, etc. Well, these stuffed animals did neither, so I would have to pretend the interaction. The need to be both the presenter and the audience made my practice sessions quite challenging, but they truly prepared me for most types of audiences.

Working hard at communicating the company message and the strategies our teams were working on made a difference, but so did the feedback I received from colleagues, my staff, and even some customers. Videotaping revealed some nonverbal habits of which I was completely unaware. The video doesn't lie, and I highly recommend it to those who want to improve their presentation skills.

Those bears, dolls, and boxes have long since found new homes. Now, as an executive, I'm in a unique position to pay all that has been invested in me forward, as well as all that I learned through my own efforts. I relish this role.

Cisco allowed me, along with a few peers, to create an internship program structured to recruit young adults to do key projects for 10- to 12-week periods during the summer months. We wanted to give the interns real work experience and for the company to benefit as well. The program grew to over 200 interns, with some incredible results on both sides of the equation. We now have a similar program at Symantec.

Late one evening I was on a video call at my desk at Cisco, and I heard a ruckus coming from the area where the interns were beginning to set up their work environment within their cubicles. When the call ended, I got up from my desk to investigate and make sure all was okay.

I discovered the interns, stacking the walls of the cubicles in a corner—during their first week at the job. They wanted to work in an open area, like a war room, where they could interact without physical barriers. They wanted to see and talk to each other all the time.

In this and many other ways, the interns reverse mentored us—the management. They gave us a priceless education with implications for productivity, innovation, and retention for the company's future. We learned the ways in which these young adults show up at work and what that means for structuring work for optimum results.

While we were learning from these young adults, they were receiving professional coaching and feedback about how to brand themselves and maneuver at work. These skills advanced them beyond their peers who only have the academic piece of the puzzle.

The internships have allowed me to invest in young adults in our family's extended network of friends. Impressed with the growth I saw as interns progressed through the program at Cisco, I began to introduce college students I know to companies that hire interns. If the kids from around the country made the effort and were hired, I began to invite a few of the extended family/friends to live with us. We now call it Jordan's Finishing School because the whole family invests in these kids. It's something we all do together.

We are conscious about mentoring while not parenting these young adults. We guide, but the kids must figure things out on their own. By the end of the internship, they have developed skills, corporate smarts, the ability to champion a point of view, confidence, and independence.

One of my favorite parts of this experience is sitting around our family's fire pit with 18, 19, and 20-year-olds, talking business concepts and solving real problems. The atmosphere around the fire pit lends itself to uncensored conversation in the same way that car talk always has for our family. We talk about weighty issues with no holds barred. I gain tremendous insights around that fire pit. It is a continuous learning experience on both sides.

Over the years, we've gotten feedback about how important the internships have been in the lives of the participants. For example, I recently learned that Gloria, one of Kim's three daughters who lived with us during an internship, has started a small mentoring group in her college. While Gloria has always been kind and supportive of others, she has now taken the next intentional step of investing in the lives of others.

* * * * *

Chances are you've heard the phrase, "Don't sweat the small stuff." The experience of being a working mom has taught me to embrace this phrase with all I am worth. For example, before I had Spencer and Jaqueline, I was fastidious about my clothes and appearance. If the dry cleaner happened to mess up an outfit or I noticed a spot, I'd be upset and hurry to change into a new outfit. Then, when the kids were babies, it seemed one of them always spit up on my shoulder just as we were rushing out the door. Eventually, I got to the point where I'd simply wipe off the mess as best I could and then wear the shadow of the stain all day.

When the world didn't end, I began to rethink some of my perspectives. I didn't want to argue over things that are unimportant, such as whether or not my kid's socks matched, when I could be making memories with them. In the same vein, I didn't (and don't) want to be fussing over minor imperfections when I could be producing results at work.

Letting go of perfection at work was a struggle for me. After all, I spent many years at Disney, where perfection is prized. Today, I think more like Apple, where new products get to market quickly and there is always a next version to improve upon the last one.

Because my 78-year-old mother can update the operating system on her phone by touching a red circle on an app labeled "update," she has a hard time understanding why my job is so difficult. I love that!

Apple has taught consumers that all versions are okay. If a certain bug isn't fixed in the current version, it will be addressed in the next version. From this, I've learned that sometimes good is good enough, and perfection is the enemy of time. I like how Amy Cappellanti-Wolf, my colleague at Symantec and mother of two daughters, puts it, "Perfection is the enemy of innovation because innovation is neither pretty nor perfect; it's how you learn. It has to be iterative, so you need to open up the space to innovate."

What a relief! And what a great lesson for the always multitasking working woman.

Having children improved my skills at multitasking and altered my perspectives on what's important. It also gave me a gift of empathy, not a natural strength for me.

As a parent, I was forced to view life through my children's eyes. From a child's perspective, "Life isn't fair" isn't a comforting response. With the kids, I learned that while the factual side of a story is usually straightforward, the way people feel about that story typically isn't. For me, parenting brought forth empathy and gentleness in ways that no other experiences could.

In our family, when the kids got in trouble, they would go to Phil first because I was prone to be more reactive. I've learned to tone that response down, take a deep breath, and give the benefit of the doubt, assuming positive intent. No matter where I am, I try to have a conversation before allowing myself to get worked up over a situation. This has made a profound difference in all my relationships.

I've had many conversations with Gwen Parks, one of my coaches, about leading for excellence rather than perfection— and about having empathy without being an enabler. I maintain high standards for myself, my kids, and my team. I am driven toward excellence, and I expect those around me to persevere through challenges. When people fail to perform, I address it, but the conversation is always about the work, not the person. We look at accountability and moving forward, not blaming or shaming. But I also think it's critical when you do make a mistake to fess up, be honest about it, own it, and apologize if necessary. The recovery of a situation can also make the relationship stronger.

Innovation and growth are stunted by blame, even as they are encouraged by accountability. Failure is a part of life, from the earliest of ages. Both leaders and parents have to guide people through it.

I've already mentioned the helpful nail-in-the-fence analogy a colleague shared with me. Another colleague taught me that almost every person we meet is currently going through some kind of personal challenge. I don't need to know what that challenge is. I simply need to remind myself that life is complicated, that people are complex packages and need to be treated with respect and empathy.

Both leadership and parenthood are about helping others to develop into the best they can be, and each role can make you better at the other. By going to work, you aren't ruining your kids. You are learning skills that can make you a better parent, especially the skills of prioritizing and problem solving. By leaving work at a reasonable hour to parent your children, you are not cheating your job. You are gaining insight into the strengths and vulnerabilities of all the people with whom you work. Don't let anyone tell you differently.

Key Takeaways

- **The job of mom complements your other job**
  On the surface, it may seem as if the job of mom is a distracter from your professional job, and vice versa. In reality, each of these jobs makes you better at the other.

- **To get the most out of every day, pay attention to how you use your time every day**
  Working parents must use every moment wisely. Consider building time into your schedule to figure out what items on your calendar you can shed or pass on to someone else.

- **Perfectionism is your enemy—let it go**
  Both at home and at work, idealized standards of perfection result in excess stress and wasted energy. Working moms must learn to let perfectionism go. This allows them to focus on deeper values, such as being fully present and investing in supportive and coaching relationships.

- **To give your best, be all in, wherever you are**
  All relationships work best when we are fully engaged. While it's not possible to be distraction-free at all times, you don't have to be your own worst enemy by trying to do too many things at the same time.

- **Accept lessons in empathy from your kids**
  Children help us to remember that even when a situation seems straightforward, the feelings around it may not be. Parenting helps us to develop empathy in ways that no other experiences can. This quality makes a mom a better manager at work.

- **PARENTHOOD AND LEADERSHIP ARE BOTH COACHING ROLES**
  Your roles as leader and parent are both about helping others to develop into the best people they can be. In many cases, the best way to accomplish this is to provide some coaching and then get out of the way.

- **ACCOUNTABILITY AND BLAME ARE RADICALLY DIFFERENT THINGS**
  High expectations are a good thing, and when someone fails, make it about the work and not the person. Innovation and growth are stunted by blame, even as they are encouraged by accountability.

CHAPTER 9

CONVERSATION WITH MY ADULT CHILDREN: PERSPECTIVES FROM THEN AND NOW

A T BABY SHOWERS, new or expectant moms receive cute—and highly predictable—gifts. For example, the mom will receive a collection of the tiniest possible clothes, even though the baby will outgrow these in a month or two (if not a week or two). She will likely get a stroller, a few diaper bags, a crib mobile, breastfeeding paraphernalia, a book about baby milestones, and the all-important book about how to get a baby to sleep through the night.

Chances are the new mom won't get a book to help her navigate her way as a working mom. If she chooses or needs to work while raising her children, the mom will have to learn as she goes. Her days will be full of trial and error, and she'll feel guilty and overwhelmed. The mom will feel that she is not succeeding at home or at work. Thankfully, there will be bright days, when work accomplishments or her children's accomplishments exhilarate her. On other days, the mom will feel utterly exhausted and torn. On those days, she will second guess everything.

I hope that someday a new mom might get this book as a gift, even if it's disguised in brown paper and slipped under the table. If I have the opportunity, I'll give the book to her myself. What's more, I'll stop by with a casserole, hold the baby, and tell the new mom in no uncertain terms that, in choosing to work, she is not about to ruin her precious child.

I'll affirm the obvious fact that she is besotted with love for her baby and will do everything in her power to give that baby the best she has to offer. Choosing to work does not negate her love and commitment to her kids.

Next, I will feed, burb, and diaper that baby while the new mom naps. If there is a little bit of spit up, I'll proudly wear it home.

As my own kids approached adulthood, I came to realize that as the kids were young and growing, I wasted a lot of energy feeling guilty about leaving them to go to work. I struggled, worrying that if I let others care for Spencer and Jacqueline, those others might replace me in the kids' minds and memories. I spent too much time pushing myself beyond my limits because I had the notion that asking for help was a sign of weakness.

I often felt guilty and feared that I might be cheating the vulnerable people whom I loved with all my heart. Both Phil and I poured ourselves into them, but I sometimes still felt torn between work and home.

As my kids matured and separated from me in healthy ways, I couldn't help but think, "Hey, I'm really proud of these kids." Spencer and Jacqueline are making their way into the world in creative and meaningful ways. They are good people with a high degree of integrity who make good moral choices, are positive and fun, and are on the road to fulfilling their career dreams. I began to celebrate the fact that I had worked at my highest levels while raising two kids, and I didn't fail at either. Sure, I made my share of mistakes, bit what human doesn't?

As you know, my intention in writing this book was to share a story of encouragement, plus a few strategies, for other working moms. In a culture full of judgment and criticism, I want to say to working moms, "It's okay; you aren't ruining your kids. You can achieve professional success and still be a good mother."

As I began working on the book, I realized that in order for the book to be credible and genuinely encouraging, Spencer and Jacqueline had to be invited to contribute. What difference would it make that I judged their lives as successful if they didn't share my view?

I'm grateful that both kids have been involved all the way through this project. They have answered my questions, read my drafts, reminded me of things I'd forgotten, and laughed as well as moaned with me over the things that didn't work out so well. Yes, we even had times where their eyes rolled back in their heads.

As you've read previous chapters, you've encountered some of Spencer and Jacqueline's perspectives on their childhood. This chapter, so near the end of the book, reflects a closing conversation I requested to make sure the book fully reflected their perspectives. I asked a few questions and let the conversation flow. So, let's hear from Spencer and Jacqueline.

When asked what they disliked and what they liked about growing up with a working mom, the answers on both sides centered on the need to think and act independently. For example, both kids have memories of school picture days. As you've read, the school photos proudly displayed in our home show that I always seemed to be traveling picture day.

School picture day was a big deal to Jacqueline, and she was sad when I wasn't available to help her get ready. She says, "If you had been home, I might not have worn that weird bracelet or so much makeup." (One year she experimented with makeup and ended up with a bit of a gothic look.) Today, however, Jacqueline recognizes that picture day rarely goes well, even when the mom is right there.

Our collection of school pictures is funny and goofy, and Jacqueline has as much fun as anyone when people visit and look at the pictures. She says, "I guess I really liked that shirt I wore two years in a row!"

Spencer remembers being a freshman in high school and being required to wear a tie for pictures for the first time. Phil and I helped Spencer choose an outfit to wear the night before picture day, but neither of us realized our son didn't know how to tie a necktie. In the morning, after a moment of "oh no," Spencer went to YouTube and followed the step-by-step video. Disaster was averted, and we thank God for video!

Spencer laughs as he tells the story—it's a good, even a proud, memory for him. He says, "I wasn't really spoon-fed. I knew I needed to have the thing tied, so I learned it on my own. Since that day, I've known exactly what to do with a tie."

When we were not going to be available, Phil and I were careful that adults our kids knew and trusted would be available. Pickup from school, hours after school, sports practices, and more were covered. The kids tell me that they often wished one of us was on pickup duty, but it was never a question of them feeling afraid or unattended. They knew they were safe and had an adult to manage emergencies.

When the kids had to do something new, we often rehearsed with them the way we rehearsed navigating an airport with Spencer when he flew by himself to get to summer camp. We are believers in age-appropriate and well-supported independence.

As Spencer and Jacqueline got older, of course, they took on more responsibility. Once, when the kids were in high school, Phil and I needed to travel somewhere by plane while the kids stayed home. I don't remember the details of the event, except that Spencer and Jacqueline were home with our new shelter puppy, Shadow. We'd had the puppy only for a short time and didn't know much about him. Jacqueline remembers that Shadow had already become Phil's favorite dog.

Just as our plane was taking off, Shadow had a seizure, and the kids called. Because Wi-Fi wasn't yet on planes, we could only talk for a few minutes, long enough for me to give a credit card number for a vet. Spencer had a driver's license, but it was still stressful for the kids to figure out how to get the dog to a 24-hour vet. Jacqueline remembers being terrified and badly wanting her parents to be there to manage the situation. Looking back, Jacqueline knows that although she was scared, both she and her brother were competent. She has never since questioned her ability to care for an animal.

*****

In our family, two working parents was always the norm. In that sense, Spencer and Jacqueline didn't know any different. Still, sometimes I wondered what they felt when they compared their family with those of their friends who had different family models. I asked, "What did you observe, and how did you feel about those observations?"

Jacqueline's first answer was more about what she reflects on now than what she noticed as a child. Some of her friends had families who fit the stereotype of the mom being the only one who cooked, cleaned, did laundry, etc. Our family never fit into those standard roles.

I acknowledge being one of the only Italians on the planet who can't cook. I honestly don't have the talent, and I envy those who do. When I start cooking, I get distracted and begin multitasking, and the cooking pays the price. My kids will say, "Mom burns soup that's already been cooked." And when the house smells like burnt toast, they say, often in unison, "Mom's cooking again." Lucky for us that Phil loves to cook and typically escorts me from the kitchen.

Jacqueline feels that the world is changing its gender stereotypes, and she's ready for it. From her perspective, there are multiple ways to configure roles between couples. She says, "I'm not stuck with a set of blinders, looking straight ahead as if there is only way things can be. I think this will help me a lot in the future when it comes to my own family and kids."

Spencer had a completely different reflection on the difference between our family and those of some friends. He said, "The biggest thing I remember about other people's parents is the importance of sleepovers."

Spencer thought sleepovers were the greatest thing. He loved the feeling of independence, experiencing different family routines, staying up late to tell stories, and seeing what the other family would serve for breakfast. He was puzzled about why some of his friends' parents wouldn't allow them to do sleepovers. As a young adult, Spencer sees the difference in parenting decisions in holding kids closer or granting more independence.

Both kids remember that our family was different—some people might say our family fell short—when it came to packing lunches. Sometimes there just weren't enough hours in the day, and while other parents packed bag lunches and inserted loving notes saying, "I love you, Peaches," we gave the children money for school lunches.

From Spencer's perspective, this was just the way it was, rather than something that bothered him. He thought it was kind of cool to eat hot lunches while other kids were eating sandwiches. He assures me, the lunches "were always funded" and the kids had money for snacks at sports practices after school.

Jacqueline remembers a difference in work ethic between us and the families of some of her friends. As you know, one of our family's guiding principles is that we work hard and play hard. I didn't want to spend my weekends doing chores while the rest of the family was playing—I wanted to spend as much time with the kids as possible. So, we did the chores together, got done quickly, and then were all free to play together. From a young age, the kids learned responsibility, accountability, and a good work ethic.

Jacqueline was notorious for trying to hide or make excuses to get out of work, but she always had to do her share in the end. Spencer understood the expectations and was less resistant. He felt a sense of pride after washing windows or spring cleaning.

Before the kids were old enough to earn money on their own, Jacqueline became aware that some of her friends could simply ask for things they wanted. She knew it didn't work that way at our house.

If Jacqueline wanted a new gadget she didn't really need, I'd give her a list of chores and say, "Complete this list of additional chores and I will pay you for the work." The kids understood reward and payment in exchange for work completed.

Jacqueline remembers the sense of pride she felt when she earned enough money from chores to purchase her own phone. She says, "At that moment, the phone was my most prized possession, not because it was a material object, but because I had worked to get it on my own."

When my daughter went to college, however, she didn't particularly like our rules about summers at home. She remembers when I sat her down and said, "You are never going to waste a college summer. You are going to work. Whether it's a seasonal job at Starbucks or an internship at a large company, you are going to work. You don't get to lie around and waste your time."

The kids utilized me as a resource for internships from a network perspective, although they had to apply and interview successfully on their own. I could get them introduced to new companies and technologies, but they needed to interview and land the job on their own merits. They needed to pursue the job, demonstrate hard work, and showcase a great work ethic daily.

Eventually, it dawned on Jacqueline that she was doing real work in companies in the field in which she wanted to work as an adult. She came to understand that my rules about summer were not just about keeping her busy; they were about preparing her for life.

When her friends from college had a degree, Jacqueline had a degree plus three summers of real-world work experience at three different companies. Looking back, she is extremely grateful for my rules about summers home from college.

* * * * *

When the kids were younger, and we utilized nannies, I sometimes struggled with having someone other than a parent care for them. Some days, leaving the kids with the nanny was gut-wrenching, especially when they didn't feel well or they begged me not to leave. I desperately *wanted* to stay home, and I felt like I *should* be staying home.

I asked Spencer and Jacqueline what those days were like for them. What was it like when they could see Phil and I were upset about leaving? Did they have confidence that we would absolutely return at the end of the day?

Spencer answered my question by sharing a memory. Our family had several nannies, and Spencer remembers when we were getting a new one. He can still picture us all sitting down and interviewing the potential nannies together. After the interviews, I asked which candidate the kids liked best, and we hired their choice. Since the kids were the ones to spend time with the nanny, Phil and I felt they should be part of the process. It's interesting to me that Spencer remembers that event so well.

On the other hand, Spencer says he has a clear memory of only one nanny among the several we had. Jacqueline doesn't have strong memories of the nannies, either, although she has friends whose nannies are a central figure in their memories.

In our house, a lot was going on in the kids' lives besides the nanny. They remember my parents, their grandparents, always being around when they were young, and they remember the times we spent together in the evenings and on vacations.

Jacqueline said, "All of our memories, like the really important stuff that we still remember 20 years later, happened with our parents." This is so encouraging considering how concerned and guilty I felt about leaving the kids. The nanny or caretaker is super important, but at least in our house, she wasn't as important as I made her out to be at the time. She wasn't my replacement.

* * * * *

The differences between the structure of my childhood home and that of Spencer and Jacqueline are significant. My mom worked as a waitress on weekends, but otherwise she was at home and raised my sisters and me. I'd see my dad for an hour or two a day, and that was it. I didn't have multiple personalities as practical role models, and I didn't get to see two parents navigate life on a daily basis.

I've always thought that having two parents with different styles raise you will broaden your perspective and your ability to see there are different ways to accomplish any particular goal. Phil and I have a great rhythm when it comes to multitasking and getting through the day, but our personalities are different—very different.

Spencer describes Phil as one of the most patient men he has ever met. Phil listens and processes what he hears. Sometimes he does provide advice in the moment, but at other times he simply listens in the moment, providing advice days or weeks later.

I, on the other hand, tend to be impatient. I am eager to fix or solve the problem in real time. I process information quickly and want to get to a quick solution. I've come to learn that sometimes the kids don't want that.

I asked the kids what these differences in style and parenting have meant for them—as children and now as adults.

Jacqueline says she developed a pattern as a child that exists to this day. "If I'm mad and I want to vent about something, I go directly to Dad and tell him whatever is on my mind. He either won't respond, or he'll offer one sentence—which is exactly what I want.

If I have an issue and I want advice, I go to Mom, no question." Having the option to vent without the intensity of parental advice (when she didn't want or need it) helped Jacqueline stay connected to a parent, rather than hiding in her room and holding it all inside where it could fester

Spencer sometimes finds Phil's few words frustrating, but if he's in some sort of trouble, he goes to Phil first. Phil calms things down and then the two of them talk to me.

Once, while Spencer was in college, he was pulled over for a traffic violation and got caught with alcohol in the trunk of the car. He wasn't drinking, but he was under the legal age for transporting alcohol. His first call was to Phil, and the two of them contacted a lawyer friend and mapped out a plan before they told me what had happened—two days later.

In that situation, Spencer knew I would have been incredibly disappointed and probably overreacted, so he and Phil handled the situation before I even knew about it. The crisis was lessened considerably by the time I was informed. Then, we were able to have a good conversation about Spencer's behavior, the mistake he had made, and his lessons learned.

If I had gotten the call first, I would have had a negative and decidedly unhelpful reaction. In our family, this was the perfect way to handle the situation.

In Spencer's mind, Phil and I wear different hats as parents. We respect each other and work together in the best interest of the kids. They know which parent to come to when. What's most important to me is that Spencer and Jacqueline have always had outlets, a parent they could go to when they felt overwhelmed, couldn't cope, or simply needed some homework or career advice. Phil and I both naturally played our roles.

I am naturally intense and quickly jump in to solve a problem. So, when Spencer found himself in Japan as a college student, facing an emergency and not knowing what to do, he called me rather than Phil. He knew I would dive right in to solve the problem.

Spencer, seizing a once-in-a-lifetime opportunity, participated in a semester at sea program, in which his floating college traveled to 13 countries in four months. Sea days were school days, and days in port were travel and exploration days. (If your child ever has the opportunity to do something like this, I highly recommend it. It is a life-changing experience. The "kids" are exposed to things they couldn't experience in any other way. They also truly learn to navigate the globe on their own.)

Spencer and 700 other students participated in his particular semester at sea. The first stop was in Japan, and the students had the opportunity to return to the ship each night or find their way to the next port days later. Not knowing anyone on the ship, Spencer connected with a group of seven or eight other students who wanted to explore Japan.

At about 6:00 a.m. California time, I got a panic-stricken call from Spencer. One of the girls in his group got really drunk on the first night, and Spencer didn't know what to do. He had just met this group of young adults and didn't know them well, nor did they know Spencer.

The young woman couldn't remember at which hotel she had registered, and Spencer was afraid to take her back to his hotel—for obvious reasons. I advised Spencer to indeed stay with the girl, give her his bed in the room he had reserved with the other guys, make sure she had her purse and other stuff, and let her sleep. The boys could take the floor and a blanket.

Spencer was happy to sleep on the floor, but he was worried the girl would wake up feeling uncomfortable with the situation and be upset with him. I said, "You just take care of her like you would any other human being, and don't worry that she will be mad about it. She will be thrilled in the morning and you guys will bond over that."

I hung up thinking, okay, that was solid advice, but I couldn't help being a bit worried. This was the first country and the first week. What else was going to transpire over the next several months? A great deal did, but that is Spencer's story for another day and another book. My point here is that, with this kind of panic call, Spencer would call me rather than Phil; I'm the problem solver in real time.

Being older than me, Phil is retired from the corporate arena now, and all four of our kids come to me for conversations about their careers. I love these conversations about how to navigate the professional world. We talk about developing strategy, negotiating relationships, managing problems, and building a career.

I get to be both mom and mentor in this arena, and Phil gets to be dad and mentor in others. Our two different styles help our kids meet challenges in different ways while feeling fully supported.

*   *   *   *   *

When I asked the kids to identify one key benefit they received from growing up with a working mom, they were quiet for a while. After all, they had never known another kind of mom. Finally, Jacqueline said the best thing was being prepared for her career.

Many things, including the ideals we instilled in the kids at young ages, have added up to the fact that Jacqueline is doing what she loves. She said, "I work at least from 9-7 every day because I was brought up knowing that this is what you must do if you want to have fun on the weekends and make a difference in the world."

Spencer agrees that being prepared for a career was helpful, but the benefit he sees stretches beyond that. He said,

"Having a mother who played in the same ballpark as my father from a professional standpoint taught us that you can do anything you want."

He continued, "Nothing should ever hold you back. If you have the drive and willpower, you can get it accomplished. Whatever you really want to do from a family or life standpoint, you can do it."

As this conversation ended, I felt both grateful and proud. I know my kids are biased, but even if I allow for that, they don't seem ruined or deeply scarred.

I'm not suggesting of course, that having a working mom automatically prepared them for successful careers or lives. As Jacqueline pointed out, many small things have added up to bring the kids to the places they are today. I'm profoundly grateful to Phil, who worked with me to instill values in their lives—and who modeled effective life and relationship skills for them. Grandparents, teachers, friends, coaches, and others also invested in our kids' lives in important ways.

* * * * *

Phil and I made our two-working-parent family work in practical ways. We modeled a fluid style in which either one of us could take on a task. I'm realizing more and more that our day-to-day realities were the *context* in which we taught them our beliefs about living successful, happy, and meaningful lives. I hope we also taught them that they have the right to define successful, happy, and meaningful on their own terms.

As you are nearing the end of this book, it's a good time to think about the principles and beliefs you want to instill in your children in the context of *your* daily life. Where do your principles and beliefs align with mine, and where do they differ? To help you answer the question, I'll summarize my guiding principles and beliefs in the next chapter. Writing this book has served to clarify them in new ways for me.

KEY TAKEAWAYS

- **OUR GROWN CHILDREN HAVE GOOD FEEDBACK FOR US**
  While all of us as parents love our children and seek to provide the best possible childhood for them, it's not until we hear from them as adults that we can know if we succeeded. A conversation with Spencer and Jacqueline about their childhoods gave me some insights I wouldn't otherwise have.

- **DIFFERENT PARENTING STYLES ENRICH A FAMILY**
  One of the jobs of a parent is to expose children to different styles of approaching life. Phil and I, very different personalities, demonstrated different approaches to accomplishing goals and solving problems. This served to broaden their perspectives while offering the different types of support they needed

- **MORE EXPERIENCES EQUALS MORE GROWTH**
  A parent's job includes providing their children with experiences that extend beyond the family's four walls. For example, in spending a semester at sea, Spencer learned more about himself and the world than Phil and I could ever teach him.

- **IT'S WISE TO INVITE GOOD ADULT INFLUENCES**
  Many things, including their own choices, add up to making our children the adults they become. Grandparents, teachers, coaches, and friends are all important influences. Whether you are a two-parent family or a single mom, invite positive and healthy people into your family's world.

- **YOUR DAY-TO-DAY REALITIES ARE THE CONTEXT IN WHICH YOUR VALUES AND BELIEFS ARE TAUGHT**

  While I believe that kids of working moms have distinct advantages, those advantages don't necessarily come automatically. The day-to-day realities of your family provide the context in which you teach your children your beliefs about living successful, happy, and meaningful lives. The more you clarify your own beliefs and values, the more likely they are to "stick" with your children.

CHAPTER 10

LOOKING BACK, LOOKING FORWARD: THE PRINCIPLES STILL STAND

IT'S HARD TO PINPOINT THE MOMENT I became passionate about parenting—probably the moment I knew I was actually going to be a mom. The love I felt when I met each of my children was so strong, it was staggering. Nothing, not even my love for Phil or members of my first family, can compare to the love I feel for my kids. At each stage of their lives, I've wanted nothing more than to be the best mom I could possibly be. I'm sure the same is true for you.

As far as work goes, I can remember taking the initiative to improve systems in my first job in high school. Working in an office for a service provider, I discovered the owner had many customers with past due bills. Knowing I couldn't be paid unless customers paid their bills, I prepared letters to be sent to move things along!

All of us spend energy on our passions, and, over the years, I've thought a lot about how to best juggle my roles as a mom and a professional. It's safe to say I have definite opinions, philosophies, and strategies for both these roles.

Refining my ideas and articulating them to you, however, hasn't been as easy as I expected. This book has evolved as it has been written, and sometimes it seemed the process would take forever.

I never intended for this book to lift me up as a role model for you or other working moms. It's *my* story—how I navigated my way through my responsibilities as a mom and a professional. I hope you've enjoyed the ride and found some connections with your own story, as well as some helpful tips. I hope you'll share your own story so that, together, we can assure working moms, "You aren't ruining your kids."

I'm on the other side of parenting now and enjoying my relationships with my adult children and my grandchildren. My love still overflows in ways that are staggering. If writing this book has done one thing for me, it has made me even more grateful for the family I call my own.

Writing has also rekindled my passions and reminded me that many of my principles for parenting and working are also my principles for living. My identity as a working mom was the context in which I tried to instill these principles and related values in my children.

At this point, I'm left with a sort of manifesto that encompasses every season of life. Here are my commitments as I go forward:

WHEREVER I HAPPEN TO BE, I WILL BE ALL IN

Life and relationships—at home, work, and everywhere else—are richest when I am fully present and engaged. Whether at a professional or pee wee sports event, I will always be the one wearing team colors and cheering loudly. If there is a foam finger to be had, I'll be the one waving it. My team members at work will call me a demanding boss, but also the one who enthusiastically invests in their development and cares most about their growth. Together, we will pursue excellence and celebrate our victories, big and small. We will also acknowledge and learn from our mistakes.

When I am at home, with extended family members or friends, I will be all in right there, working hard, playing hard, listening carefully, and giving my full support.

WHEN IT COMES TO OTHERS JUDGING MY FAMILY, I'LL RESERVE THE RIGHT TO ACCEPT OR REJECT

In celebrating my family in these pages, I'm not suggesting we are perfect—just that we are a family and have the right to forge our own path as such. The marketing and media ideal of the perfect family is fabricated rather than real, and I reaffirm my commitment not to compare my family to that ideal. We are silly and competitive and proud to be ourselves.

I'm aware that in writing this book, I may be criticized by those who have different views. That's okay. I'm just telling my story, not telling anyone else how to behave.

I'LL LOOK FOR THINGS TO LET GO, RATHER THAN FOR THINGS TO TAKE ON

There will always be more opportunities than time and more spaces to keep clean and organized than any working mom can manage.

When Spencer and Jacqueline were little, I looked for things to let go of in order to give myself space to be fully present for them. At my current stage of life, my mom, who live hundreds of miles away, needs attention. Sadly, I lost my dad during the writing of this book. Other priorities pale in the face of the short time with have left with the parents who mean so much to us.

I will continue my Sunday night practice of reviewing my professional calendar for the upcoming week, looking for things to shed. For example, if several IT people from my team are in a meeting, I don't need to be there. In other instances, I will step out of the way so that someone else can grow professionally.

The more I grow as a person and a leader, the more I focus on living for impact rather than activity. I want my time to count.

I'LL ASK FOR HELP

It took me too many years to give myself permission to embrace my strengths and outsource the things that others can do better. None of us is good at everything, and we drain our energy when we insist upon forcing ourselves to try.

I'm been fortunate to have a husband who partnered with me in managing daily parenting tasks, and my parents were invaluable helpers when Spencer and Jacqueline were young. I understand that not everyone has these advantages.

I was fortunate to grow into a salary that allowed me to hire some additional help, but giving myself permission to ask for help was essential, before and after that was true. Money isn't the deciding factor in getting help—attitude is. Carpooling, shared babysitting, and many other solutions are about trading, bartering, and creativity. I built wonderful relationships with my neighbors in Florida as we worked together to manage our parenting tasks when our kids were in elementary school. No family needs to be an island or feel alone.

I'LL SEEK TO INTEGRATE ASPECTS
OF MY LIFE RATHER THAN BALANCE THEM

I become indignant when I hear the term work/life balance. Balance implies the ability to allot time equally in a way that simply doesn't exist in the real world. Life is too messy for balance; one side is always heavier than the other, and you often can't predict which side will be heaviest on any given day. The only solution is integration while being on the lookout for red alerts that your kids need you to step out of your professional role and focus entirely on them.

I will continue to think of work as a verb and believe that everything in life is negotiable. I will continue to use technology to help me juggle my various roles.

I'LL CHOOSE THE BIG PERSPECTIVE OVER THE BIG REACTION

Life is full of stresses, mistakes, missteps, and disappointments. How we react to these not only affects our moods but the moods of those around us. Especially with young kids, if no one is getting hurt and nothing irreplaceable is getting broken, I'll choose to respond with humor as often as possible. When humor isn't the appropriate response, stepping back to look at the big perspective usually will be.

At work, where mistakes or unforeseen circumstances sometimes cause big, expensive problems, I'll still choose the big perspective. While I'll hold my team members accountable, I won't focus on blame—and certainly not on shame. I'll help my team members to dig in and fix the problem. Then, we will do a critical assessment together and learn from the experience. This practice of critically assessing events and experiences is one of the professional skills I've intentionally brought home to my kids.

I'LL INVEST MY ENERGY IN QUALITY TIME
AND NOT WORRY SO MUCH ABOUT QUANTITY

If anything triggers guilt in working moms, it's the issue of not being there for their kids *always.* In fact, being available for every issue your kids face can hinder their growth into independence.

Since I can't be with the ones I love always, I will be all in when I am. I'll remember that it isn't *what* I do with my loved ones, as long as we do something together. Chores and errands can bring as much togetherness as playtime, as long as everyone is fully engaged.

At this stage in my life, I am especially aware of the limited time I have with my aging mom. Sometimes, the highest quality time with her is simply sitting, disconnected from all my electronics.

I'LL TREAT FAMILY CELEBRATIONS AND VACATIONS AS SACRED

In our family, the path to high-quality time has always included protecting celebrations and vacations against all other priorities. I will continue to invest my energy and creativity into planning these events and enjoying every minute we have together.

As Spencer and Jacqueline get older and make families of their own, while Shannon, James, their spouses, and our grandchildren follow their own dreams, getting everyone together will get more challenging, but it will always be a priority. The kids tell me that Phil and I have taught them the value of sacred family time well, and I look forward to precious hours together.

I'LL MAINTAIN OPEN LINES OF COMMUNICATION, EVEN ABOUT UNCOMFORTABLE TOPICS

Our years of "car talk" with Spencer and Jaqueline are over, but that doesn't mean we don't need to build space into our lives to talk. Technology makes it easy to touch base frequently, but technology doesn't encourage deep sharing. Only time spent together can do that.

I will nurture a family culture in which we talk openly, even about sticky problems, misunderstandings, and failures.

My favorite venue for deep sharing is our New Year's Eve dinner, in which we each reflect upon the past year and discuss our accomplishments, things we wish we could do over, and our plans for the coming year. We also talk around the family fire pit, which has a special magic for triggering meaningful conversations.

* * * * *

As I come full circle in this book, I remember my opening story about 2-year-old Jacqueline hanging on me, sobbing and begging me not to leave her to go to work. I remember how awful I felt about having to leave and my surprise when I peeked in the window 10 minutes later. There was Jacqueline in the midst of a circle of kids, laughing. She was fine.

So here is the lesson: By leaving Jacqueline in a safe place while I went to work, I was not ruining my child. In fact, even at age 2, she was learning age-appropriate independence and social skills.

When I got home from work that day, as I did routinely, I showered Jacqueline and Spencer with my love, giving them the sense of grounding and security that all children need. Of course, on some days, work responsibilities required some adjustment, but I was religious about setting boundaries that allowed me to pour love into those kids with quality time. The structures changed as the kids grew, but the commitment never did.

I am convinced that being a working mom helped me become a better parent, and being a parent helped me become a better leader. My kids appreciate the skills of prioritizing, problem solving, task management, and continual improvement that I modeled and taught along the way. My team members appreciate the empathy and appreciation of different perspectives I learned from interacting with my kids.

It turns out that by being a working mom, I was not ruining my kids or cheating my job. I was enhancing my performance in both areas.

Chances are that as a working mom, you sometimes (perhaps often) feel torn between home and work. The media fabrications of the ideal family don't help. I encourage you to embrace the positives, celebrate your victories, and shed the guilt. I'm standing on my soapbox and shouting so that you and all other working moms can hear:

YOU ARE NOT RUINING YOUR KIDS!

ABOUT THE AUTHOR

SHEILA JORDAN is Chief Information Officer at Symantec, where she has set the IT vision and strategy, developed an experienced leadership team, and insourced IT operations by building Symantec's next generation secure data center in the company's virtual private cloud.

She was named CIO of the Year, innovation and transformation category, in 2015 by the Silicon Valley Business Journal for leading the effort to split IT operations when Symantec separated its security and information management businesses.

Prior to joining Symantec, Sheila held senior leadership positions at Cisco Systems and The Walt Disney Company.

In the face of many professional and personal accomplishments, Sheila is most proud of her four grown children, Shannon, James, Spencer, and Jacqueline. While building her corporate career, Sheila, along with her husband, Phil, was intentionally raising their children, pouring love into them, teaching core values, and helping them build skills for living successfully.

Sheila believes working moms, rather than cheating their children, provide special advantages, especially in the areas of prioritizing, problem solving, and time management.